W9-BJI-574

BIOSPHERE 2

A WORLD IN OUR HANDS

The classroom biosphere and other lessons about
how Earth's biosphere works

D.A. SIELOFF

THE BIOSPHERE PRESS ™ • Oracle, Arizona • (800) 992-4603 • Biosphere 2, A Division of Decisions Investments, Inc.

In an old cloth notebook—scribbled with words—smudged soil, and samples of algae globs, camphor, and frankincense dash the pages. It's where I worked, preserving the prose of scientists and translating most into tools for educators. My notes and experiences inside Biosphere 2 lent greatly to the spread of learning material in this book.

Before joining Biosphere 2, I worked with corporate America training teamwork concepts to manufacturing and engineering personnel. Some of the problem solving exercises were modeled after Biosphere 2. Hundreds of professionals have been through these courses. Then, in August 1993, I stood in front of Biosphere 2 for the first time, and remember most its enormity. Biosphere 2 is unlike any other world I have known. Under the expanse of the far-reaching spaceframe, Biosphere 2 seems larger than the life it embraces. This laboratory acknowledges the scientist, the philosopher, and the technologist, as well as something Edward P. Bass (Chairman of the Board, Decisions Investment Corporation, parent company of Biosphere 2) refers to as "the human endeavor."

It takes teams of people, the best science has to offer, to meet the challenges of Biosphere 2. Life in this laboratory changes, moves, and surprises even the most astute and patient observer. High in the upper savannah—above the coconut, the macadamia, the bamboo, the morning glory, and the mangrove the thorny frankincense sits. Its branches reach like many arms out over the ocean to those who look into Biosphere 2, the world of learning. It is appropriate to explore learning in such a fashion, reaching out to meet the challenges, the unknown. May you find *Biosphere 2: A World In Our Hands* a practical, challenging endeavor.

— *D.A. Sieloff*

COPY EDITOR
Marilyn Martin

ART DIRECTION & GRAPHIC DESIGN
G.D. Dundas

PRODUCTION MANAGER
G.D. Dundas

PRODUCTION ASSISTANT
Kathy Horton

ILLUSTRATIONS
Kathy Horton

Cover Design by G.D. Dundas

PHOTO CREDITS
Gonzalo Arcila, Bryce Canyon National Park, Phil Dustan, Russ Finley, Matt Finn, Tim Fuller, Gill Kenny, Tom Lamb, Linda Leigh, Tilak Ram Mahato, Pascale Maslin, Scott McMullen, Peter Menzel, C. Allen Morgan, Adalberto Rios Szalay, SBV, Karen Silva, Matt Smith, Don Spoon, NASA, Yosemite National Park.

TECHNICAL & SCIENTIFIC ACKNOWLEDGEMENTS
Bruno D.V. Marino, Ph.D., and Robert Edison, Tony Burgess, Ph.D., Matt Finn, Lynette Fleming, Ph.D., Marilyn Martin, Joanne Pifer, Robert Scarborough, Donald Spoon, Ph.D., Shirley Sokol, Josh Tosteson.

Copyright © 1995 Biosphere 2. All rights reserved.
Printed in the United States of America by Arizona Lithographers
on recycled paper using soy based inks.

FIRST EDITION
ISBN 1-882428-27-7

Dear Colleagues:

What is Biosphere 2 and what is unique about the facility? Biosphere 2 allows one to discover aspects of the world anew and to observe a synthetic but living ecological entity; it is a living laboratory for studies of the earth and ecology. The scale of Biosphere 2 is large enough to engender complex interactions between plants and soils, for example, but small enough to acquire a complete, holistic view of the system. Biosphere 2 is the only facility of its kind anywhere. Scientists and professionals of many disciplines come together at Biosphere 2 to think creatively about environmental problems that are relevant to our contemporary world and that demand our attention. Students are encouraged to use Biosphere 2 in the same way, that is to extend their knowledge of the planet.

Biosphere 2: A World in Our Hands curriculum provides a way to combine aspects of many disciplines in a creative manner and synthesize applicable knowledge that motivates and captures the intellectual imagination of the students. This book should provide impetus for rigorous study of many basic science themes that very likely have been addressed in classes in the past. Students should find application of their knowledge stimulating and rewarding.

Section One of the curriculum introduces the facility itself. Through text, maps and numerous photographs each of the ecologically distinctive areas (i.e., desert, rain forest, savannah/thornscrub, marsh, ocean, and agricultural areas) is described allowing teacher and students to experience the dimensions and unique structural, architectural, and biological features of Biosphere 2. The Biosphere 2 facility is cast as a unique laboratory to study the biology and ecology of the earth from a new experimental perspective. In Biosphere 2, features of the earth that would require trips to many parts of the world are within reach for observation and, more important, for experimentation. Learning the basics of biology, ecology and other related disciplines in the context of Biosphere 2 should allow the student a genuine learning experience that captures the essence of science and research activities. The ultimate goal is to use Biosphere 2 as a tool to extend our understanding and appreciation of contemporary environmental issues.

Dr. Bruno D.V. Marino
Director of Science and Research
Biosphere 2

Section Two amplifies many of the basic science concepts motivated by discussions initiated in Section One. The vital concept of energy as a source of planetary radiant heat and light for photosynthesis of the global biota is needed to conceptually link the basic functions of Biosphere 2 with Biosphere 1(Earth). Suggestions for discussions and follow-on activities are presented for each topic. Use of outside references and resources to elaborate on particular themes is encouraged.

Section Three examines a number of features of Biosphere 1, particularly the important cycles of water and other elements that again can be studied in both the world around us and in Biosphere 2. The comparison of features of the water cycle, biology of coral reefs and the ocean, the carbon cycle, food chains, soil dynamics, plant function, etc., between Biosphere 2 and Biosphere 1 should provide a rich intellectual milieu for learning. The same format of suggested discussions and activities used in Section Two is used here to focus on each topic. The experiments suggested are almost all carried out with simple "home ingredients," allowing any teacher the opportunity to engage students in hands-on, basic science activities.

Section Four suggests a six-part activity in which a small scale "biosphere" is constructed in the classroom from a variety of simple materials. This exercise is designed as a team effort that requires discussion, identification of specific research goals, and some experimentation with the apparatus. Elements of the subjects touched upon in the earlier sections can now be articulated by the students. Measurement of temperature, for example, over a period of time could be compared with plant activity and light conditions. In essence, the students should learn well that changes or actions in one variable can initiate a series of related reactions, or feedbacks, for the entire biosphere. Illustration of interrelation of factors in the "class built" biosphere with discussions of how such feedbacks could occur in Biosphere 1 and 2, should provide a life-long message to the student.

Good Luck!

Bruno D. V. Marino, Ph.D.

CONTENTS

Contents

continued

SECTION 3: The Biosphere (cont'd.)

SECTION 3: The Biosphere (cont'd.)

SECTION 4: The Classroom Biosphere

GLOSSARY OF TERMS:

REFERENCES:

APPENDIX A: Biosphere 2 Posters

6

OBJECTIVE: The Classroom Biosphere was designed to assist sixth-to eighth-grade students and their teachers with achieving the type of scientific literacy advocated by Project 2061, which considers that "the natural and social sciences, mathematics, and technology are so closely linked that curriculum for them should not be developed separately." The Classroom Biosphere educational series can help learners use scientific skills and ways of thinking to actively study the world as described by mathematics and shaped by technology.

THINKING STRATEGIES: Students will engage in dialoguing, creative thinking, planning, identifying, connecting, recalling and forming questions, as well as setting goals, evaluating progress and summarizing results.

EXPERIENTIAL ELEMENTS: Science can be fun and challenging. This book contains the essential elements for small-scale biospheric design and study. Students work in teams, as do members of the Biosphere 2 project, to research, plan, construct, monitor, measure and analyze data. Students gain an understanding of how their decisions impact the performance of the system they design through discussions, hands-on experience, reading, research, data collection, and data analysis. The general design of this program is to encourage creativity within a general framework.

SCIENCE SKILLS: Participation in this program can help students:

- Gain an understanding of the global or local impact of science and technology on ecological systems that are complex and not always predictable.
- Cooperate with other students to find answers and solve problems.
- Rely on data, facts and observations.
- Become willing to modify explanations.
- Explain phenomena using scientific explanations.
- Gain an understanding of organization, cause and effect, systems, models, change, structure and function, diversity, and interactions.
- Understand that scientific and technological achievements build upon one another.
- Plan and conduct controlled experiments to test hypotheses.
- Employ decision-making skills.
- Use imagination and creativity, and formulate questions about nature to solve problems.
- Gain hands-on experience in conducting explorations and investigations.
- Collect, organize, and analyze relevant data, draw and apply reasonable conclusions, and assess components of the experimental design.
- Identify instances of scientific concepts in everyday life.

BIOSPHERE 2. . . HOW THE EARTH WORKS: The word *biosphere* comes from two Greek words: *bios*, meaning life, and *sphaera*, meaning ball or globe. Biosphere is the part of the globe within which life can exist. The only biosphere we know of is that of Earth's, Biosphere 1, where life exists in a thin layer around the planet.

To help us learn more about how Earth's biosphere sustains life, Biosphere 2 was built. Biosphere 2 is essentially materially closed and informationally and energetically open. Inside, there are five wilderness biomes, all from warmer regions of Earth. A rain forest, savannah, desert, marsh, and ocean are included in the 3.15-acre spaceframe-and-glass laboratory. Also, there is an intensive agricultural area, micro city, and technosphere.

Both living and nonliving components play a part in maintaining the delicate balance of life inside. Science and technology are used to simulate, manage, and monitor, as closely as possible, the cycles and conditions which exist in Biosphere 2. Air content, circulation, leakage, and recycling; humidity and thermal levels; water recycling, rainfall, ocean movement and water quality; and waste recycling are examples of processes and characteristics supported and studied through the use of Biosphere 2's technological resources.

PEOPLE WORKING & LEARNING: Biosphere 2 is a 100-year research project that is possible because people work together. The teams of scientists and technologists at Biosphere 2 are composed of individuals with diverse backgrounds who contribute to the total program. This educational package emphasizes cooperation, communication, and critical thinking through a series of activities that encourage imagination and creativity, as well as brainstorming, reasoning, consensus building, sensing, researching, and decision making.

CONCEPTS: The purpose of research is to ask and answer questions using controlled and rigorous procedures in order to test hypotheses, discover facts, and construct increasingly accurate models of the world. The concepts in this program include scientific research, systems (ecosystems, recycling, water cycles, carbon cycles, etc.), cause and effect, models, change, organization, diversity, interactions, structure, and function. Students should understand the close link among the natural and social sciences, mathematics, and technology. They should see how the scientific community uses interdisciplinary teams to execute experiments, solve problems, and expand the body of knowledge regarding Earth's biosphere.

THEMES: Themes in this program include *The Nature of Science* (based on inquiry and enriched by interdisciplinary perspectives and cooperation), *Patterns of Change* (the natural world and its recycling systems), and *Effects of Our Actions* (relationships between science, technology, society, and the understanding of our relationship with the environment).

SECTION

Biosphere 2

Biosphere 1 is Earth's biosphere, a thin layer around the planet where life exists. Biosphere 2 is a laboratory designed to study global ecological issues and promote a better understanding of the earth's biosphere. The space frame-and-glass apparatus is the most tightly sealed structure of its kind (with a leakage rate of 10 percent per year). The steel and concrete liner cradles miles of technology that supports the scientific research inside Biosphere 2.

Biosphere 2 was designed as a materially closed ecological and environmental research project. It is open to energy and information flow. Its purpose is to help us understand how the earth works. Inside there are five wilderness biomes, all from warmer regions of Earth. This 3.15-acre laboratory has a rain forest, savannah, desert, marsh, and ocean with coral reef, as well as an intensive agricultural area, micro city, and technosphere.

DISCUSSION

OBJECTIVE:

To introduce students to the Biosphere 2 project.

MATERIALS NEEDED:

Overhead projector • overhead transparencies of photographs (Appendix A) or make wall displays.

PROCEDURE:

1. Color photographs of Biosphere 2 and its biomes are contained in Appendix A. Cut them out of this book and prepare a wall display.

Note: An optional way to present the visuals is to have color overhead transparencies made and presented to the students with an overhead projector.

2. Review the Biosphere 2 information on pages 10 - 27, and become familiar with the information and sequence of images you will present to the students.

3. Encourage discussion in the classroom. Ask students to share what they know about Biosphere 2 and the global ecology questions this laboratory could help solve in the future.

4. Show the Biosphere 2 image to the students and discuss:

Show students this Biosphere 2 image.

Biosphere 2 is a long-term research project designed to last 100 years. It is possible because people work together. The teams, composed of people from many areas of expertise, contribute to the total program. Scientists admit there are many mysteries about how life on Earth stays in balance. That is one reason Biosphere 2 is so important. It's a teaching tool: a place to learn how life maintains balance, to solve the mysteries and discover ways to take better care of Earth. Questions for scientific inquiry include:

- How to sustain life.
- How to maximize food production without harmful chemical fertilizers and pesticides (which can get into the drinking water and air).
- How to restore endangered ecosystems like rain forests, estuaries, and coral reefs.
- How to recycle all air, water, and waste in places where we live and work.

The science is possible because of advanced technologies developed for the support of the project, including electronic systems, computer software, construction and sealing technologies, and others.

10

11

Basic Biosphere 2 facts:

Size: 3.15 acres (1.27 hectares)

Volume: 7.2 million cubic feet (203,760 cubic meters)

Spaceframe: 20 miles (32.2 kilometers)

Panels: 6,600 panels of 3/4-inch glass, plastic, and glass laminate

Wilderness Biomes: Ocean, rain forest, marsh, savannah, and desert

Artificial Areas: An intensive agricultural area, a micro city and a technosphere

Species: 4,000 originally thought; now scientists believe there are more

Energy Requirements:
• Sunlight
• Electricity

Global Monitoring System: 1,000 sensors inside download into a 5-tiered data processing system

Emergency Systems: Biospheric Operations' automated systems scan Biosphere 2 critical factors every 15 minutes via sensors

Other Automation: Temperature control, wave machines, water recycling, waste recycling, air current/wind/circulation, rain and water flow

Each hour nearly 4,000 pieces of information can flow from Biosphere 2 to Biospheric Operations, which includes information transmitted via personal computers, telephones, and digitally transmitted video conferences

12

Biosphere 2
rain forest.

5. Show the students the image of the **Biosphere 2 Rain Forest** and discuss:

How would you build a laboratory to study global ecology? What tools would you need? What would you include? How realistic could it be? These are the questions that faced teams of scientists and technologists in the 1980s when Biosphere 2 was only an idea. The scientists decided to replicate very productive ecosystems found on Earth—tropical and subtropical. One type of ecosystem included in this laboratory is the rain forest.

There are tropical and temperate rain forests on Earth that, through their biodiversity, contain great biological wealth, such as medicines, foods, and petroleum substitutes.

The large rain forests also consume large quantities of carbon dioxide which many refer to as a greenhouse gas. (Carbon dioxide acts like the glass in a greenhouse, allowing some solar rays to pass through and reflecting outgoing thermal radiation.) *What other atmospheric benefit do you think we get from rain forests?* (Pause and encourage student answers.) Oxygen production. Earth's atmosphere is 20.8 percent oxygen.

Global ecologists, concerned about the loss of Earth's rain forest population, continue to research the environment. Scientists estimate that approximately 55 percent of Earth's rain forests have been destroyed by human activity, and the loss continues at a rate of about 100,000 square kilometers (38,610 square miles) per year. Loss means extinction for some species that cannot migrate fast enough to escape loggers, farmers, and cattle ranchers.

The Biosphere 2 rain forest has many of the same characteristics as the rain forests of the world. Rain forests, characterized by densely populated forests, have layers, such as:

Show students this rain forest image.

- **TALL TREES (40 METERS HIGH)**
- **THE CONTINUOUS CANOPY (18-24 METERS/59-80 FEET HIGH)**
- **THE MIDDLE LAYER OF SHADE-LOVING TREES (12 METERS/39.4 FEET HIGH)**
- **THE UNDERSTORY (PALMS, SHRUBS, SAPLINGS)**
- **NON-WOODY HERBS**

13

Biosphere 2 rain forest understory.

The typical rainfall in this type of ecosystem is more than 2,000 mm (78.8 inches) per year, with a mean annual temperature of 86 degrees F.

Computers maintain the rain forest temperature in Biosphere 2 in the range of 90 to 105 degrees F (32 to 41 degrees C). Computers control the rainfall, too. The humidity inside Biosphere 2's rain forest is controlled by technology. Foggers run throughout the day and night. Experiments and research being performed on the water cycles in the rain forest include analyzing what happens when moisture moves through the soil, evapotranspires from plants, and goes back into the air.

Biosphere 2 research includes restoration studies. Scientists are examining the impact of climatic change on rain forests, how species interact with the environment, and more. The research may lead to a better understanding of how to restore damaged forests—a very complex task.

Technology provides the fog over the rain forest mountain in Biosphere 2.

14

Show students this savannah image.

6. Show the students the image of the **Biosphere 2 Savannah** and discuss:

Prehistoric beasts once roamed the great savannahs. Charles Darwin called the ancient African grasslands "the cradle of life." Archaeologists agree. Modern work of scientists around the globe has unearthed ample artifacts and fossils from the grasslands—the savannahs.

Natural grasslands occur where the rainfall is between that of the desert and that of the forest lands. Biosphere 2 has an upper savannah that winds down to the lower savannah where water pools in the water-logged soil. The Biosphere 2 savannah, too, is located between the desert and the rain forest.

Biosphere 2's grassy savannah represents a tropical-type savannah, where rainfall is generally 60 inches (1,524 mm) per year. Large grasslands occupy the interior of the North American and Eurasian continents. Australia, Africa, and South America possess vast grasslands, as well. The dominant life forms are the grasses which can range from very tall grasses of five to eight feet, to shorter grasses of six inches or less.

Scientists say the well-developed grassland communities contain species with different temperature adaptations. That is, some grow in the summer heat, and others in the cooler winter months.

Nongrassy plants, such as herbs, trees, and shrubs also grow in savannahs, often in belts where streams or rivers run. Biosphere 2's savannah has a stream up near the trees. The acacia tree has an umbrella-like shape. *Can anyone name the types of wild animals that graze the Earth's grasslands?* (Encourage students to name the grazing animals.)

Elephants, antelope, bison, deer, kangaroo, birds—large and small—are grazers, and they depend on grasslands for food. Some are runners, but some burrow. All compete for shrinking territory with domestic relatives: goats, cattle, and sheep.

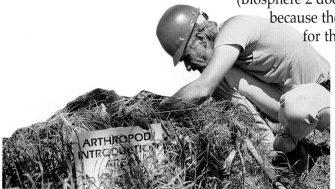

(Biosphere 2 does not have large grazers because the 30-foot cliff is too dangerous for the animals.) Additional threats to wild grasslands include replacement by domesticated plants: primarily corn and wheat sown into the ground by human hands.

Hands-on science in Biosphere 2's savannah.

Biosphere 2's savannah features many grasses and trees collected.

The earth's grasslands represent about 23 percent, nearly one-fourth, of world land area used by humans. The percentage of land usage was, at one time, much higher. Grasslands and forested areas, converted to cropland, comprise another 11 percent of world land use. Global ecologists believe the current rate of overuse of grasslands, especially those converted to grazing and cropland, could lead to increased desertification if the trend continues. Many of the world's desert ecosystems cannot support the life forms of the grasslands. Once an ecosystem converts into a desert, it is difficult to restore the species and soil fertility without resorting to technological support with large energy needs.

Biosphere 2's savannah was started from scratch. Researchers defined the soil needs, created a number of soil blends, and imported specific savannah plants from Australia, Madagascar, South America, and North America. Engineers designed and installed technologies to carefully manage the temperature and water requirements of the savannah.

Research continues in the savannah to learn more about the interrelationships between the savannah and its neighboring desert and rain forest biomes in this ecological project. Species adaptation, growth levels, survival rates, water consumption, atmospheric interactions, and other characteristics are being studied.

Savannah construction in Biosphere 2. A stream runs through it.

16

Show students this image of the desert.

7. Show students the image of the **Biosphere 2 Desert**, and discuss:

The water sprinklers simulate rain inside Biosphere 2. Computers run the automated watering system, based on the requests of the biome managers, to create seasonal changes.

In 1991, the desert biome looked very different. The moisture, which travels through the air in this laboratory, has caused the desert to evolve into a thornscrub.

Various technologies are used in the desert to monitor the environment.

This desert has species from coastal fog deserts. These species can tolerate high levels of moisture in the air around the seas. The desert plants have evolved to their environment and can survive long periods of drought, if necessary, too.

The desert in Biosphere 2 experiences heavy growth during the winter months—a time when the other biomes in the glass laboratory are less productive. The growth process produces oxygen inside Biosphere 2. Therefore, the desert growth produces oxygen during the months when the other biomes slow down.

Plant growth leads to the production of oxygen and the consumption of carbon dioxide. The leaves, stems, trunks, and roots store the absorbed carbon. The oxygen level in Biosphere 2 is around 19 percent, (Earth's oxygen level is 20.8 percent). The carbon dioxide averages 1,000 parts per million—although it is higher at night than during the day. (Earth's carbon dioxide level is 350 parts per million). Most buildings contain 2,000 to 5,000 parts per million, without the circulation of fresh air. Dangerous levels for humans are close to 10,000 parts per million.

Scientists at Biosphere 2 study carbon dioxide consumption and oxygen production; two aspects of the photosynthetic process in plants.

Scientists collect desert species for Biosphere 2.

The desert biome is an important biome in a laboratory for global ecology. *Can anyone tell me why?*(Encourage answers from students.)

Desert biomes take up great areas of land in Africa, Australia, South America, the Far East, Central America, and a portion of North America. There are many species in the desert that are beneficial to humans and other animals that have evolved and adapted. Several ancient cultures existed for thousands of years on the food sources available in the Sonoran Desert—where Biosphere 2 is located, for example.

There is a difference between deserts and desertification of land that has many global ecologists concerned. Overused land and infertile soil prevent many crops from growing. Loss of natural habitat presents another problem when humans move in and change the face of the land. *Can you think of other problems?* (Encourage students to recall the rain forest presentation.)

A loss of biodiversity can be a problem. Species cannot adapt to their new environment or migrate to a more compatible area. Even desert ecosystems face threats such as change in species and soil conditions. Desertification threatens 3.3 billion hectares (8.15 billion acres) of land, from overcultivation,overgrazing, rapid growth of human populations, cutting or deforestation, and inappropriate irrigation that changes the land and sometimes the climate. The research in Biosphere 2's desert includes research on the struggles for territory between species of neighboring biomes and the desert species.

Species struggle for soil space in the desert.

18

8. Show the students the image of the **Biosphere 2 Marsh,** and discuss:

The Biosphere 2 marsh is the most sophisticated laboratory-contained marsh available to scientists. Marshes, estuaries, and wetlands are important in global ecology. Marshes act as large filters between the terrestrial (or land) biomes and the marine systems and oceans. The soil and heavy nutrient drainage overwhelms the fragile life that exists in oceans, lakes, ponds, and large rivers. They cannot survive the intake of rich nutrients, directly. Marshes are nutrient-rich.

Show students the Biosphere 2 marsh. The section dividers separate the sections by salinity. The freshest water is in the foreground.

The Biosphere 2 marsh represents a form of marine system called an estuary—a type of marsh that generally starts as a freshwater marsh at its inland location, and increases in salinity the closer it gets to the ocean. The Chesapeake Bay and the Florida Everglades are two estuaries located in the eastern part of the United States. Both are experiencing environmental change due to human abuse.

What do you think is causing problems in the Everglades? (Encourage responses from the students.) Pollution from industry, tourism, increased residential construction, and human use bring problems. A shrinking habitat and estuaries overloaded with debris and pollution cannot perform their function effectively. Damage to the marshes causes problems for the wildlife living there, not to mention the rivers, lakes, and oceans that receive the overflow of debris and pollution.

Biosphere 2's marsh biome represents 20 miles (32.18 kilometers) of Florida Everglades. Inside Biosphere 2 it is condensed into 200 feet (61 meters). The food web in the wilderness marsh is too complex to synthetically duplicate. Teams of scientists from Biosphere 2 and the Smithsonian believed the best approach was to go directly to the source: Florida. The Biosphere 2 marsh is the only biome in which species were brought in from only one site. The scientists dug up the plant species, soil, microbes, insects, water, and all . . . right out of the Florida Everglades.

DID YOU KNOW?

Estuaries on Earth experience tides? Biosphere 2 does not duplicate the tidal movement inside. The experiments up to this date have not required the use of tidal simulators.

Collecting marsh species from the Florida Everglades mangroves.

Section dividers in the Biosphere 2 marsh split this biome into six areas. Each section represents a distinct set of conditions that change from **fresh** to **salt** water typical in an estuary. The Biosphere 2 mangroves are white mangroves, red mangroves, and black mangroves. Inside the marsh biome, these three varieties occupy different sections of the marsh and do not compete for root space. They do compete for sun light. *What do you think causes this condition?* (Encourage answers from the students.) The salinity levels change from one section to the next. The section closest to the Biosphere 2 ocean has the heaviest salinity. Most terrestrial plants cannot survive high level of salinity in their environment.

Scientists use technology to manage and monitor the key characteristics in the Biosphere 2 marsh. They make adjustments as needed so that the environment stays within critical parameters. It rains every day in the freshwater marsh. Biosphere 2 technologists recycle all the water in Biosphere 2 after it has been processed through a desalination machine which removes salt. Even so, Biosphere 2 personnel continually check the salinity levels and make adjustments as needed to ensure a healthy environment in the marsh.

Marsh system research at Biosphere 2 includes projects inside the apparatus and outside in the Biome Ecology Laboratories (located on the Biosphere 2 campus) and in the Florida Everglades. The parallel studies provide a way to compare and contrast Biosphere 2 data. For example, Biosphere 2's analytical chemists monitor gas (and other chemical) exchanges and look for clues as to what role the marsh systems play in the complex study of Earth's biosphere.

Working in the Biosphere 2 freshwater marsh.

20

9. Show students the **Biosphere 2 Ocean** image and discuss the following:

Biosphere 2 features the largest man-made ocean of its type in the world. It contains 900,000 gallons (3.41 million liters) of simulated ocean water made from a mixture of fresh water, Instant Ocean (a commercial mix), and real ocean water trucked in from the Pacific Ocean.

This ocean has two parts: the open ocean and the lagoon, a sheltered area beyond the barrier reef. The basin of the ocean is 25 feet (7.6 meters) deep, the lagoon about 10 feet (3.1 meters) deep. With the help of technology, this ocean has waves. The ocean water temperature is programmed to stay between 75 and 82 degrees F (24 to 26 degrees C).

Show students the Biosphere 2 ocean.

Biosphere 2 technologists apply automation in the ocean biome. Technology controls the wave and temperature variations, monitors chemistry, and measures water quality and water levels. The temperature is manually controlled. A series of sensors send signals to the Biospheric Operations' command room, where computers process the readings and send signals when the ocean changes beyond the programmed parameters.

What would you want scientists to study if you had a million-gallon ocean to build? (Pause and encourage students to provide answers. Do not correct any of the suggestions. Repeat each, and ask for additional ideas.)

Many people think Biosphere 2 has sharks or whales or dolphins in its ocean. It does not. These are large animals, and they require large open spaces with plenty of food sources. The Biosphere 2 ocean is a self-sustaining system, like the other biomes, driven by the energy of the sun and artificial light. Food supplements, as you would expect in an aquarium, are not part of Biosphere 2. Scientists are studying how the earth works, and oceans—not aquariums, which are more for entertainment and educational viewing—provide the scientific information we seek.

The life forms inside this ocean include many kinds of algae. The blue-green algae is one of the oldest known forms of life—possibly 3. 4 billion years old. Biosphere 2's ocean has blue-green algae in it. The algae are necessary to the ocean—they are near the bottom of the food chain and integral to the food web.

Top of the food chain in the ocean is the dolphin — a creature too large for Biosphere 2.

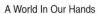

Algae, too, play an important role in oxygen production. Algal scrubbers are used in Biosphere 2 if the algae levels get too high.

About 65 million years ago, coral reefs could be found in most of the earth's oceans. As the land masses changed, so did the positions of the coral reefs. Today, the living reefs exist in the tropics. Coral reefs are beautiful ocean systems, home to many species of colorful coral and fish. The biodiversity of the reefs has attracted a great deal of attention from scientists. Fish and coral species are spectacular members of our ocean community. The great beauty of the reefs attracts tourists by the thousands. Many countries, such as Australia and Central America, have reaped great economic benefits from coral reef tourism.

Scientists have identified threats to the health of the world's coral reefs, including pollution and misuse stemming from such activities as tourism, industry, soil erosion, shipping, and fishing industries—great problems whether looked at separately or combined. Loss of coral reefs could be a large problem in Earth's future. *Why?* (Encourage students to discuss the problems.)

A reduction in the quantity of the world's coral reefs might correlate to a reduction in the number of living things in the oceans. The fluctuation of the living systems on our planet and their geochemical environment might mean a great change in our ocean diversity. In essence, the balance could be thrown off. Loss of species might mean extinction for many, loss of food sources for some—which might in turn affect the quality and quantity of food available to human populations.

Biosphere 2 provides a unique, controlled area for ocean systems study. It is a place where we can gain a better understanding of the world's reefs. More important, it may yield information on how the earth works.

Sea anenome: elegant ocean life in Biosphere 2.

10. Show students the image of the **Biosphere 2 Intensive Agricultural Area** and discuss:

The Biosphere 2 Intensive Agricultural Area does more than feed the crew. It is a research area as well. Methods in soil management, fertilization, pest control, high-yield crops, and species diversity are a few of the issues horticulturalists, agronomists, and others raise and are studying at Biosphere 2.

Show students the intensive agricultural area image.

Biosphere 2 is a closed system. Harmful fertilizers or pesticides are not permitted inside. *Why do you think this policy is important?* (Encourage responses and interact with the students.) The harmful chemicals recycle and pollute the air and water systems. Biosphere 2 recycles the air, water, and waste. Eventually the chemicals could end up in the drinking water, in the food, and throughout the biomes in the animals, plants, and microbes.

Biosphere 2 research is looking at ways to expand our understanding of the planet. We are researching species productivity and genetic diversity, under the Biosphere 2 house rules:

- No pesticides except oil and soap that are biodegradable.

- No fertilizers except ones that are biodegradable and organic.

Biosphere 2 research includes reviewing new plant-growing methods, companion cropping, and plant-based pest control solutions. Parallel studies get conducted

Sorghum crops inside Biosphere 2 are grown in the Biome Ecological Laboratories simultaneously.

inside the Biome Ecology Laboratories (BEL), located in separate facilities at the center of campus. The BEL is maintained under ambient gas concentration (air). They have the same seasons and light regimes as Biosphere 2. In both places, scientists experiment with plants that repel other plants' pests, organic solutions for pest control, and crop production. For instance, before introducing a new variety of beans into Biosphere 2, a similar plot is planted and maintained in the BEL. Scientists collect and compare data acquired from the two research facilities, trying to identify similarities and differences in the rate of growth, maturity, and yield.

Technologies, such as growing lights, have been used during agricultural studies in Biosphere 2.

Many people believe species diversity is important, especially when pests grow increasingly resistant to pesticides and crops increasingly lose resistance to disease because of genetic limitations. Many people believe the disease resistance of domesticated crops is not as great as that of the wild variants.

Through the years people have grown nearly 3,000 varieties of plants for food. More than that are edible. *How many plant species do you think are edible on this planet?* (Encourage students to respond.) More than 72,000. Agriculturists concentrate on about 150 plant species on a large scale around the world. Also, 75 percent of human nutrition comes from 7 crop species. They are: corn, rice, wheat, sorghum, barley, cassava, and sweet potato. Wheat, corn and rice represent 50 percent of all large scale farm crops—3 human-created hybrids from wild species.

Researchers analyzed more than 156 plant species for Biosphere 2's first mission in 1991. New crop research continues in the Biosphere 2 facilities. The work is intensive, and continues to aggressively approach the subject of biological controls, fertility, species diversity, and productivity. For example, outside Biosphere 2, it takes an average of 4 to 8 acres (1.6 to 3.2 hectares) of land to feed one person with fruits, vegetables, milk, eggs, and meat. In Biosphere 2 scientists learned how to feed a crew of up to eight on less than 1 acre (1.4 hectares) using available energy.

The Intensive Agricultural Area hosts a number of technologies used in various studies: growing lights (used during certain conditions), which increase the light intensity over the crops, watering systems, and ground and air composition sensors, to name a few.

Biosphere 2's global agricultural work could be put to use in areas where food production is limited, malnutrition is prominent, or low crop yields impact the quality of life. The effects of droughts and famines could be reduced through the new methods that may be developed at Biosphere 2.

Corn in Biosphere 2's intensive agricultural area.

24

The micro city.

11. Switch to the **Biosphere 2 Micro City** image and lead a discussion on human made biomes:

Cities are one of the artificial environments worthy of study in global ecology. The very word artificial has a creative implication: contained in the word *artificial* is the word *art,* to create. The ancient Greeks' model of the city, or *polis,* stood for a dynamic but stable system that was in balance with nature and grew manageably.

Experts say that most modern cities are not in balance with nature. The growth in the majority of cases is explosive, not managed. The explosions take their toll on the planet's health. In many developing societies, ecological planning and policy are void; growth, expansion, and consumption are without a system of checks and balance. For example: Bangkok experienced growth levels that devoured 3,200 hectares (7,907 acres) of farmland (an area the size of Manhattan) each year for 10 years. Streets, structures, and pollution replace healthy natural habitat. Problems with air quality, waste management, water quality, transportation, and energy are often rampant when population growth explodes. When designing Biosphere 2, the managers carefully regarded the delicate balance of the environment and the number of people and types of activities allowed inside in order to avoid "urban" problems of pollution and overcrowding.

The micro city in Biosphere 2 can accommodate a specific number of people. It has apartment facilities for up to 10 residents and can accommodate more visiting scientists inside Biosphere 2 for less than 1 day. Biosphere 2 crews fit into four types of categories:

- **Alpha:** long-term mission/core crew (six months to one year)

- **Beta:** short-term mission (one to three months)

- **Delta:** short-term mission (less than one month)

- **Gamma:** Less than one day (no overnight stay)

DID YOU KNOW?

Typical American Household Waste

(Percentage)

Paper and Cardboard	30%
Organic Material	30%
Glass	10%
Metal	10%
Other Materials	12%
Plastics	8%

How much waste does the average American throw out in packaging each month? Enough to equal his/her own weight.

Dining in
Biosphere 2.

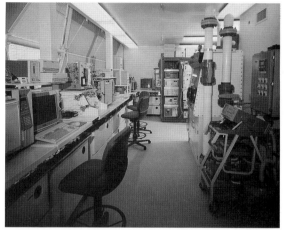

The laboratory.

The library.

Biosphere 2 designers gave a great deal of considera-tion to the human factor. The micro city serves the needs of the crew and researchers with a variety of facilities. It took years of research, review, and (sometimes) redesign before managers decided upon the most productive, environmentally friendly equipment and materials. The Biosphere 2 team worked very diligently on the micro city to ensure that all aspects of its design and construction addressed and incorporated environmentally friendly materials. Advanced sensing technologies (called the global monitoring system) are employed to monitor human impact on the biological, geological, and chemical balances inside the project.

How would you design a micro city? What would you want in there? (Encourage the students to respond.) The micro city inside Biosphere 2 has:

- A laboratory with equipment that does not emit toxic gases.

- A command room with computers and electronic communication systems.

- A medical facility for minor medical treatments.

- Kitchens: Biosphere 2 has two kitchens for meal preparation. Food is refined in the processing kitchen and cooked in the second kitchen.

- Apartments for up to 10 people. There are 5 bath-rooms, so the Biospherians and scientists share facilities. Each apartment has a library downstairs, and a separate bedroom upstairs.

- A dining area: A large dining table accommodates the researchers at meal time and provides space for meetings.

- Laundry facilities: Several electric washers and dryers are in the Biosphere 2 laundry room. Because all water is recycled, the soaps have to be biodegradable.

- A library & observatory: Five stories up in the tower is the library and observatory.

12. Show students the Biosphere 2 image again, and discuss some of the history of biospheric research, as well as the research at Biosphere 2:

In 1926, Vladimir Vernadsky, a Russian biogeochemist, wrote: "The surface of the Earth, seen from the depths of infinite celestial space, seems to us unique, specific and distinct from that of all other heavenly bodies. The surface of our planet, its biosphere, separates the Earth from its cosmic surroundings. . . The Biosphere is the only region of the Earth's crust where life is to be found. . . There is no force on the face of the Earth more powerful in its results than the totality of living organisms. The more one studies the Biosphere the more one is convinced that in no case are its phenomena disassociated from life. . .

"If life were to disappear it is obvious that the great chemical processes would likewise disappear, at least on the surface of the Earth. All the minerals in the upper layers of the crust, such as clay, limestone, chalk, ores of iron and aluminum and dozens of others, are continually being created under the influence of life.
Should life disappear, the elements of these minerals would form themselves into new compounds and . . . the known minerals would irrevocably disappear.
There would be no force on the Earth's crust capable of perpetually giving birth to new compounds . . ."

Vladimir Vernadsky, author of *The Biosphere*.

Earth receives energy from the sun which fuels many of the biogeochemical processes in the biosphere.

"The perpetually active forces of the biosphere, the heat of the sun and the chemical action of water, would not effect much change, for, with the extinction of life, free oxygen would disappear and the quantity of carbon dioxide would be greatly diminished . . . Water, also, is a powerful chemical agent, but it must be remembered that this activity is due to life, chiefly microscopic organisms.

"Chemically pure, "dead" water is a substance of indifferent chemical activity compared with natural water.

"Without life, the face of the Earth would become as motionless and inert as the face of the moon.

"Life, therefore, exerts a powerful permanent and continuous disturbing effect on the chemical stability of the surface of our planet. With its colors and forms, its combinations of vegetable and animal organisms and the creative activity of civilized humanity, life not only creates the whole picture of our natural surroundings but penetrates into the deepest and most grandiose processes in the Earth's crust "(source: *The Biosphere*).

Biosphere 2 is, perhaps, the only facility that addresses the biological, geological, and chemical interactions on the planet on such a large scale. It provides a unique laboratory setting for scientists to study the parts, the subsystems of the earth, and then tie those studies back to the whole system.

28

OVERVIEW: This activity challenges students to employ reading, communication, writing, and analytical skills in a cooperative learning environment.

OBJECTIVE: Students gain an awareness of the relationship between science and technology at Biosphere 2.

MATERIALS NEEDED:

Copies of press release (see page 29) • dictionary • paper and pencils

PROCEDURE:

1. Explain to the students that Biosphere 2's Public Affairs Office sends news and facts to reporters who write their stories or film the broadcasts for newspaper, television, or radio.

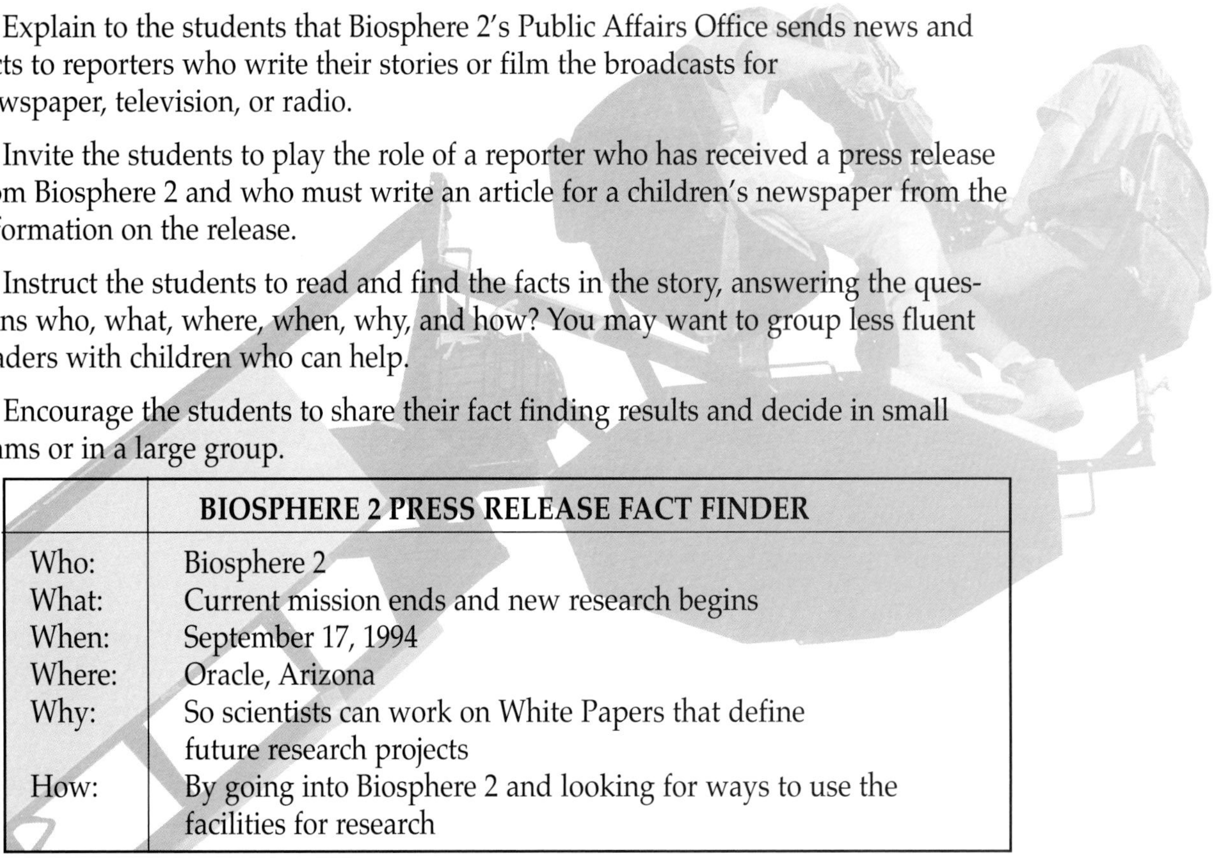

2. Invite the students to play the role of a reporter who has received a press release from Biosphere 2 and who must write an article for a children's newspaper from the information on the release.

3. Instruct the students to read and find the facts in the story, answering the questions who, what, where, when, why, and how? You may want to group less fluent readers with children who can help.

4. Encourage the students to share their fact finding results and decide in small teams or in a large group.

BIOSPHERE 2 PRESS RELEASE FACT FINDER	
Who:	Biosphere 2
What:	Current mission ends and new research begins
When:	September 17, 1994
Where:	Oracle, Arizona
Why:	So scientists can work on White Papers that define future research projects
How:	By going into Biosphere 2 and looking for ways to use the facilities for research

5. Provide the students with a way to play the role of science reporter and articulate their interpretation of the story based on the facts derived from the fact-finding activity. Invite them to write a story. Tell them to include all of the facts. Ask them to write in newspaper style. It may be helpful for students to provide examples of newspaper stories in class for reference. You may want to limit the story to one page.

Suggested Assessment

Children should be able to articulate the essence of the story derived from the Biosphere 2 press release and include all of the facts from the fact-finding activity.

CURRENT MISSION TO END ON SEPTEMBER 17, 1994
Consortium Scientists Begin Work in Biosphere 2 to Create Science Plan

Oracle, AZ—The current mission in Biosphere 2 will officially end on Saturday, September 17, 1994. Until the re-entry, a full contingent of "Gamma" crew members (short-term residents) will rotate through the apparatus.

"Most of the short-term residents doing work inside the Biosphere from now until September 17 will be scientists who have been commissioned to write white papers, that will define specific areas of research Biosphere 2 is uniquely equipped to address," said Stephen K. Bannon, Acting CEO of SBV, the parent company of the Biosphere 2 project. "It is important for the scientists to have a hands-on experience with the resident operating crew inside Biosphere 2 so they can see how the apparatus operates during a mission. The white papers will be the foundation for the project's long-term science plan."

Scientists and engineers going into Biosphere 2 as short-term residents will work on engineering systems upgrades and on developing the science plan. On Monday, August 22, 1994, Dr. Robert Russell, Director of Human Services of the Human Nutrition Research Center on Aging at Tufts University, who will be writing a white paper on human nutrition and metabolism, Dr. Bruno D.V. Marino, formerly of Harvard University, Director of Science and Research at Biosphere 2, and Gary Hudman, Chief Engineer at Biosphere 2, will enter the apparatus.

Three SBV staff members entered Biosphere 2 on Monday, August 15, 1994, as a Gamma crew for one week. This Gamma crew is paving the way for future visits by preparing preliminary operations manuals for the apparatus. They are former Biospherian and recently appointed Terrestrial Wilderness Manager Linda Leigh; Scott McMullen, Biospheric Operations; and Biosphere 2 videographer Ren Hinks.

Leigh will produce instructional documentation for the Terrestrial Wilderness ecosystems. "I'm delighted to be back with the project," she said. "I devoted two years of my life to living inside Biosphere 2, and it's like a homecoming for me. I'm sure my experience during Mission One is going to prove to be valuable during this assessment." McMullen will be formulating biospheric operations manuals for the apparatus. Hinks will document operational activities for future biospheric training tapes.

This is the fourth Gamma crew to enter Biosphere 2 since April 1. Biosphere 2 and Columbia University's Lamont-Doherty Earth Observatory announced on Sunday the formation of a new consortium, a non profit joint science venture. Besides generating a long-term scientific plan, the research group will establish a full-scale Biosphere 2 Research Institute, a consortium of major universities, research institutions, and national laboratories.

Following the current mission, a transition period of approximately seven months is planned to give access to scientists, engineers, and researchers who will determine the scientific direction of the project.

SECTION 2

Energy

31

The sun's energy is the input that drives the biogeochemical processes in the biosphere. The output is the heat produced by the processes.

A biosphere works as a system. The earth's biosphere is open to energy input and output. It receives its primary energy from the sun. The earth is also a fission device and produces a flux of heat from within. The biogeochemical processes that occur in the envelope around Earth are driven by the sun's energy. The output is heat. This section focuses the student's attention on the "input" component of the biospheric system: the sun.

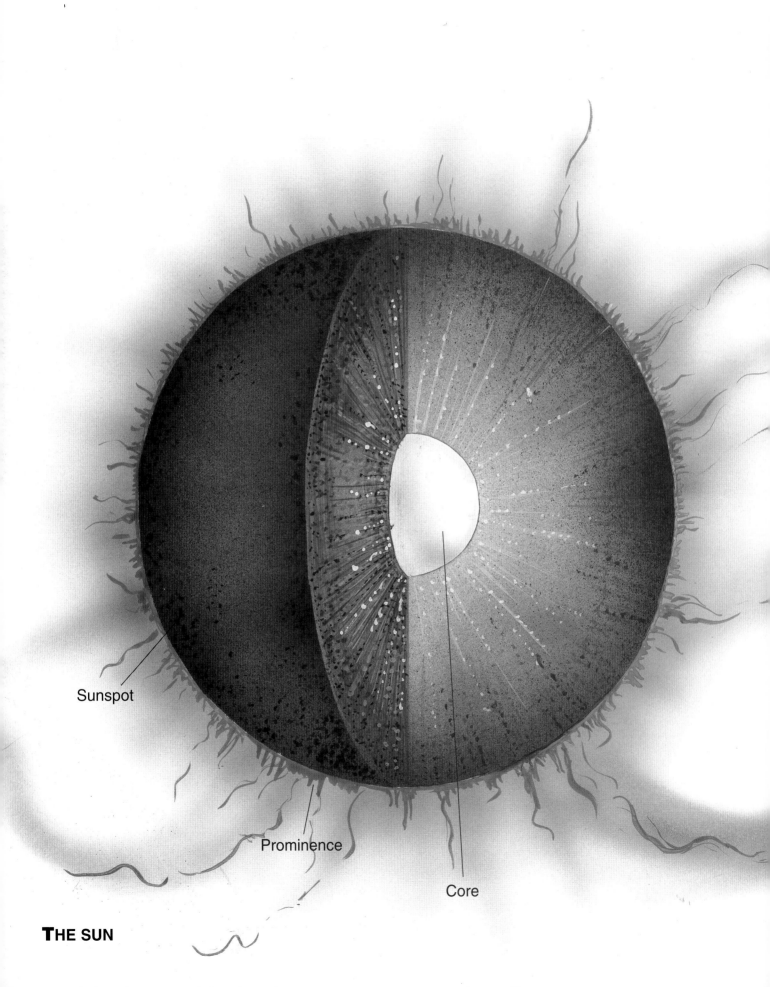

Sunspot

Prominence

Core

THE **S**UN

OBJECTIVE: Students gain an awareness of the electromagnetic spectrum and solar radiation.

PROCEDURE:

1. Lead a discussion based on the following: Scientists believe that life would not exist in Earth's biosphere if it were not for energy from the sun. The sun is about three-quarters hydrogen and one-quarter helium.

Solar radiation is a form of energy. It travels from the sun to the earth in small waves (between 0.1 and 10 micrometers). Light—made up of packets of energy called photons—travels in a straight line. Sunlight (like all electromagnetic waves) travels to Earth's biosphere at a rate of 186,000 miles per second (nearly 300,000 kilometers per second). Sunlight, or solar radiation, provides an energy input which causes interactions to occur between the living and nonliving systems of Earth. The biological and chemical processes, fueled by the sun, produce heat of their own—like the hot breath of an animal respiring, the heated desert, or the heat in our muscles when we do work.

2. Draw a chart of the electromagnetic spectrum. Show students where solar radiation falls on the spectrum.

33

ACTIVITY

Sunlight provides free energy in Biosphere 2.

OBJECTIVE: Students identify the sun/solar energy component of the biospheric system.

MATERIALS NEEDED:

Paper • pen or pencil

PROCEDURE:

1. Ask the question: *Can you name another example where the sun's energy (the input) drives a process that produces heat as a final output?* (Encourage students to provide answers.)

2. Challenges students to draw a flow chart of the input, process, and output.

ACTIVITY

The Electromagnetic Spectrum

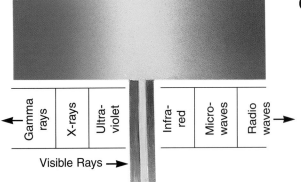

← Gamma rays | X-rays | Ultra-violet | Infra-red | Micro-waves | Radio waves →

Visible Rays →

OBJECTIVE: To encourage students to search for evidence of solar energy in their world outdoors.

PROCEDURE:

1. Organize students into teams.

2. Invite students to work in teams to identify living or nonliving things in which sunlight (energy) drives a process and produces heat.

3. Challenge students by making a contest between teams to find the largest number of examples where sunlight produces heat on or in an object.

4. Invite the teams to present their findings to the class.

Visible light and the spectrum of colors from space.

OBJECTIVE: Students explore the concept of wave-type energy.

PROCEDURE:

1. Lead a discussion with students based on the following:

Solar radiation has several bands of visible light (we see things with this light) and two invisible parts: ultraviolet light and infrared light. The electromagnetic spectrum includes both visible and invisible light. Both varieties of light travel as wave-type energy. Light from the sun is 45 percent visual, 10 percent ultraviolet, and 45 percent infrared (or heat) energy. When the ultraviolet and visual light strikes an object, the object gives off some visual, but mostly infrared nonvisual light.

Plants reflect the green and near infrared light waves. Scientists and technologists, knowing this fact, developed satellite remote sensing technologies to use these spectral bands to capture patterns in vegetation, the conditions of crops (such as healthy, diseased, flooded), etc. Plants absorb blue and red visible wavelengths, the far infrared, and to lesser degrees, the green visible and near infrared wavelengths. This part of the spectrum is the PAR or "photosynthetically active radiation."

The infrared light produces the "heat" we feel. A wave of infrared light is longer than a wave of ultraviolet light. Many different objects emit infrared rays in the form of thermal radiation. The hotter the object, the stronger the infrared rays and the greater the thermal radiation.

Biosphere 2, located near Tucson, Arizona, is in one of the sunniest locations in the U.S. to take advantage of the high levels of sunlight. Why? Because the team in charge of building Biosphere 2 knew the sun's light was "free" energy for plant growth. Often the temperature outside Biosphere 2 reaches 110 degrees F (43 degrees C) in the summer. Inside Biosphere 2, the thermal radiation (captured under the glass panels) can cause temperatures to reach dangerous levels for life (up to 150 degrees F/66 degrees C).

2. Tell students that Biosphere 2 has a four-system Energy Center. Each of the four systems would have to fail at the same time in order for the cooling to be lost and life in Biosphere 2 harmed. Ask the question: *Why is it important for Biosphere 2 to have many backup systems for heating and cooling as the sun's energy levels change?* (Encourage students to discuss the heat magnification inside the glass structure.)

Inside Biosphere 2: a rainbow.

35

OBJECTIVE: Students gain an understanding of the cause and effect of solar radiation on objects in a biosphere.

The Energy Center produces electricity, much of which is used to run the heating and cooling systems that maintain the temperatures in Biosphere 2.

36

MATERIALS NEEDED:

Thermometer • paper • pen/pencil

PROCEDURE:

1. Discuss examples of how energy travels from a source (sun) to a detector (object).

2. Instruct students to measure the temperature of the air. Record the temperature.

3. Invite students to compare the temperatures of different objects set in direct sunlight with the temperature of the air in the room (ambient temperature).

4. Invite students to compare the temperature difference between similar objects growing in direct sunlight and in shade.

5. Ask students: How many times greater is the temperature of the object in direct sunlight than that of the shaded object?

6. Lead a discussion to encourage students to describe the variations in thermal radiation found in the various objects they examined.

Solar radiation causes the heat to build quickly in Biosphere 2. Here are the cooling towers. Water is cooled, then moved through pipes to chill the air. Cool air is moved through Biosphere 2 by an air handling system.

37

OBJECTIVE: To help students gain an awareness of the interaction of the sun (energy) with the biological components (living things) of the earth's biosphere.

MATERIALS NEEDED/EACH TEAM:

Plastic bags (3) • one dark paper bag • pea or bean seeds (12) • thermometer • ruler • water • paper towel • tape • paper • pencil

NOTE: This activity requires access to a refrigerator or comparable cold chamber (such as an ice chest with a layer of insulation between the ice and seeds).

PROCEDURE:

1. Lead a discussion with students: Plants need sunlight, air, water, and minerals to live and grow in Earth's biosphere. In the right heat, with air and water, seeds can sprout. If the seeds are too cold or too hot, chances are they will not sprout. Most seeds can sprout without light. Each part of the plant works to keep the plant alive and growing. The leaf uses energy from the sun. It draws in carbon dioxide from the air. The leaf needs water and raw minerals, which it gets from the roots. Sunlight drives the process of photosynthesis by which plants manufacture sugars in each leaf. The plant's leaves, stems, and roots transport the sugars through the rest of the plant all the way to the roots, to fuel growth and the work involved in respiration and transpiration.

2. The word *photosynthesis* means that the plant takes light (photo) and changes the chlorophyll, carbon dioxide, and water into sugars (synthesis). Instruct students to write the two words separately (*photo + synthesis*), then together (*photosynthesis*).

3. Put students in teams and distribute materials. Explain that this experiment shows how thermal radiation influences seed germination (sprouting). Students should compare the effect of warm versus cold locations instead of light versus dark on the germination rates.

4. Soak three pieces of paper towel in water. Put four pea seeds in each piece of moist towel.

5. Label one bag "Sun," the second bag "Covered" and the third bag "Cold." Write the date on the bags. Label the paper bag "Covered."

6. Put the seeds in their towels inside each plastic bag.

7. Put the bags marked "Sun" and "Covered" in a warm, sunny location. Place the bag marked "Cold" in the refrigerator (or other location with the temperature maintained near 35 - 40 degrees F / 1.6 - 4.4 degrees C).

8. Assign a time each day for five consecutive days for the students to check the seeds. Invite the students to record any changes in the seeds, such as the date of germination, growth, and death. Record the temperature and light intensity (i.e., sunny or cloudy day). Take a baseline reading at day one, and record changes through day five.

NOTE: Monitor students' records to ensure they remember to record critical information.

9. Encourage students to combine written records with illustrations (e.g., number, size, germination date, survival problems, etc.).

The intensive agricultural area includes research in germination and survival rates.

Most seeds can sprout without light. Students should compare the warm versus cold locations instead of light versus dark on the germination rates.

10. Invite student teams to present the results of their investigation through formal or informal presentations, classroom discussions, or written papers. Students should address:

• Did any seeds sprout? How many sprouted in each bag? Which bag had the largest sprouts? The smallest sprouts?

• Why the seeds sprouted differently in the different locations, using the data collected during the experiment.

• Why the surviving sprouts survived, and what factors could have determined extinction.

The sorghum crops in Biosphere 2.

Assessment Suggestion

Students should be able to cooperate and correlate temperature (source: solar radiation), air, and water with successful germination at the end of this experiment.

Phototropism in
Biosphere 2.

OBJECTIVE:

To introduce students to the concept of
phototropism and the cause and effect
relationship between the sun and the
plant hormone auxin.

MATERIALS NEEDED/EACH TEAM:

Alfalfa, mustard or grass seeds (10) • small growing pot or tray • potting soil
• water • recyclable polystyrene or paper cup
(opaque or black) • ruler • pin • paper • tape • pencil

PROCEDURE:

1. Lead a discussion of phototropism: Plants do not have brains, however, a chemical
called auxin acts much like a brain. Auxin (a plant hormone) flows through the plant
from the root tips and stem, where it is produced. Auxin reacts to gravity and light. The
greatest production of auxin is in the terminal tips and the youngest leaves. From there,
auxin goes through the plant and sends signals through the plant cells.
These signals cause the leaves to move to face the sun.

2. Explain to students that the word phototropism has two parts: *photo* (light) + *trope*
(move toward). Invite students to write *photo + trope* and then *phototropism.*

3. Explain that green plants need light from the sun to manufacture food, and that this
experiment shows how plants grow toward the brightest light source.

4. Instruct students to sow the seeds in moist soil in the growing pot.
Sow the seeds in an area smaller than the diameter of the cup.

5. Teacher: Sow seeds in moist soil in a growing pot, as in step 4, for use in step 11.

6. Place the pots in a warm, sunny location. Keep the soil moist. Do not over water.

7. Monitor the growth of the seeds. Record when each sprout appears. When five or
more sprouts have grown one inch tall, have students prepare an illustration that
shows the shape and direction the sprouts are growing.

39

VOCABULARY EXERCISE

Explain to students that the word
phototropism has two parts:
photo (light) + trope (move towards).
Invite students to write ***photo + trope***
and then ***phototropism.***

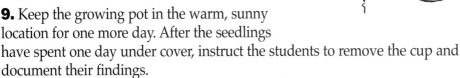

8. Punch small air holes in the base of the cup using the pin. Position the cup over the top of the seedlings.

9. Keep the growing pot in the warm, sunny location for one more day. After the seedlings have spent one day under cover, instruct the students to remove the cup and document their findings.

10. Instruct the students to make one hole the size of the pencil diameter in the side of the cup. Place the cup over the seedlings. Put a piece of tape on the growing pot exactly under the hole in the cup (for purposes of orientation to see if the seedlings grow toward the light source/hole).

11. Teacher: Place a solid cup over your seedlings. Do not puncture the cup. Use the seedlings in your cup as a baseline for students to compare with their seedlings and understand the phenomenon of phototropism.

12. Check the soil, and water the seedlings if needed. Return the seedlings to the warm, sunny location for two days. Orient the holes in the cup toward the brightest sunlight.

13. Invite students to predict what will happen to the seedlings in your cup and the seedlings in the cups with holes.

Vines in Biosphere 2 growing toward the light.

14. Instruct the students to remove the cup positioned over the seedlings. Invite them to document their observations (i.e., what happened to the seedlings, and what caused the change).

15. Ask students to prepare a written explanation of their findings. Encourage students to incorporate graphics (illustrations, charts, etc.) to support their analysis.

Assessment Suggestion

Students should be able to present an explanation of phototropism.

A scientist conducts research on photosynthesis in the Biosphere 2 marsh biome.

OBJECTIVE: To develop an awareness in students that biodiversity accounts for variations in phototropic characteristics.

MATERIALS NEEDED:

Notebooks • pencils

PROCEDURE:

1. Invite students to explore an outdoor location. Arm them with notebooks and invite them to document their observations. Encourage students to look at the diverse shapes of the plants, the shapes of their leaves, as well as the direction in which the plants bend (if at all, do they bend toward the light source?).

2. Encourage students to use drawing skills, as well as writing skills to prepare their field notes.

41

Layers of the Biosphere 2 rain forest receive different levels of light.

3. Challenge students to search for evidence that plants need sunlight to grow. Ask them to compare plants in sunny locations, shaded locations, and small plants under trees, shrubs, or other larger plants.

NOTE: Often an open location and a location where a large tree grows offer contrast in density, direction, and robustness of growth, especially where grasses grow.

4. Describe the relationship between the biological systems and the nonliving components.

5. Challenge students to answer the following questions:

• What caused the various plants to grow in different directions?

• What caused similar plants to grow differently? Was it primarily sunlight, or was it amount of water, age, soil quality, gravity, or other factors?

Assessment Suggestion

Students should be able to draw conclusions from their observations and correlate their findings regarding plant species diversity, status of health, physical location, direction of growth, and shape to energy availability.

42

Sample Field Research Data Sheet Format

Date: ————————————————————

Time: ————————————————————

Field Research ————————————————

Evidence of Microbial Activity ——————————

Ecosystem (Forest, field, desert, rotting log, rock, etc.)	Evidence of Decomposition	Organisms (leaves, dead animals, insects, worms, fungus, etc.)

OBJECTIVE: Students analyze global issues related to the energy needs of human society and energy sources.

MATERIALS NEEDED:

Paper • pencils

PROCEDURE:

1. Invite students to prepare written responses to the discussion outlined in step 2 below. Ask students to listen to the problem description and:

• Identify the environmental problem in one sentence.

• Identify the cause of the problem in one sentence.

• Identify the consequence of the problem in one sentence.

• Describe a possible solution to the problem, and why each student feels that way.

NOTE: Adapt the following discussion to fit your students' abilities.

2. Lead a discussion based on the following: Sunlight provides an energy input which causes interactions to occur between the living and nonliving systems in the earth's biosphere. Humans can capture the energy in sunlight and convert it to electricity. Christopher Flavin (Earthwatch Institute Vice-President, Research) wrote: "The world is swept each day by an abundance of renewable energy, most of it derived from the sun. Wind power, biomass energy, geothermal power, and solar energy itself could run a highly energy-efficient economy many times over. But practical problems remain. . . . The electricity they generate is hard to store—suitable for many applications but not for running an entire economy. While oil can be moved from remote areas by tanker, and coal can be transported by barge, sunshine is hard to carry to distant cities" (*State of the World, 1992*).

3. Challenge students to prepare written responses. The purpose of this activity is to provide a platform upon which students can graft new knowledge to an older framework and write about how they know what they know.

4. Not all students will approach the last question in similar fashion. Students are individuals. Expect the results to be diverse as well.

Assessment Suggestion

Students should focus on the environmental issue related to solar energy and the problem of storage and transportation. Students should be able to analyze the problem and recommend a conceptual solution in a clear, concise manner. Students should be able to examine and communicate how their knowledge and/or attitudes influence their perspectives.

The energy needs of Biosphere 2 are met by the Energy Center.

43

SECTION 3

The Biosphere

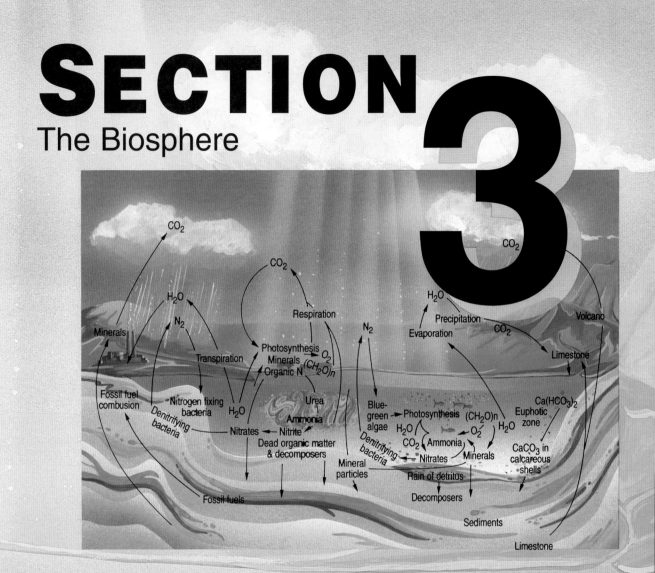

Within the illustration the following labels appear:

CO_2 · CO_2 · CO_2 · CO_2

H_2O · N_2 · Minerals · Respiration · Volcano · H_2O · Precipitation · Evaporation · Limestone

Transpiration · Photosynthesis · Minerals · $(CH_2O)n$ · Organic N · O_2 · N_2

Fossil fuel combusion · Nitrogen fixing bacteria · Denitrifying bacteria · H_2O · Urea · Ammonia · Blue-green algae · Photosynthesis · $(CH_2O)n$ · Euphotic zone · $Ca(HCO_3)_2$

Nitrates · Nitrite · H_2O · CO_2 · Ammonia · O_2 · H_2O · Minerals · $CaCO_3$ in calcareous shells

Dead organic matter & decomposers · Denitrifying bacteria · Nitrates · Minerals

Mineral particles · Rain of detritus

Fossil fuels · Decomposers · Sediments · Limestone

Earth's biosphere or Biosphere 2 requires a consideration of the processes that occur within the system. As mentioned in Section 2, the sun provides energy and fuels the biogeochemical processes in the biosphere. The biological, geological, and chemical interactions are critical and are related to the events that have sustained life on the planet for billions of years. This illustration depicts a contemporary version of the interactions of cycles in the biosphere including industrial and agricultural interactions driven by humans. Scientists continue to work toward an understanding of the relationships between the cycles and processes at Biosphere 2 in order to gain a better understanding of how the earth works. The activities contained in the following pages represent a sampling of ways to explore the interactions between living and nonliving things in the classroom and outdoors. Students can benefit by thinking about the biospheres—Earth's and the laboratory, Biosphere 2—before getting into the specific exploration activities. The information on the next two pages is for your reference.

45

Earth's biosphere.

Biosphere 1: Earth

Size: Diameter at equator is 7,926 miles (12,756 kilometers).

Age: Scientists believe Earth's crust solidified around 450 to 470 billion years ago. The oldest microorganisms may be nearly 3 to 4 billion years old. Therefore, Biosphere 1 is at least 3 to 4 billion years old.

Atmosphere: Approximate depth is 400 miles (640 kilometers). The troposphere is closest to Earth, and extends about 7 miles (11 kilometers) above Earth. It contains most of the gas in the atmosphere on which life depends. It also contains 98 percent of Earth's water (in vapor form).

Oceans: 70.8 percent of Earth's surface. Average depth is 2.2 miles (3.5 kilometers). The oceans formed billions of years ago when Earth's molten surface cooled, volcanoes erupted and spewed water vapor, and the rain fell, filling hollows and basins around higher land masses.

Land Mass: 29.2 percent of Earth's surface. Crust depth is up to 44 miles (70 kilometers). Soil is one of Earth's most valuable resources. There are many types of soils, from dry desert soils, loose sand, and packed clay, to watery mud and thick silt. Soil forms from the wearing (weathering, oxidation, etc.) of rocks into small particles. Some soils take hundreds, thousands, even millions of years to form. Some soils are a combination of minerals and decayed organic matter such as leaves, insects, and animals.

46

DID YOU KNOW?

In order for the biosphere to exist, life (bios) had to exist. With the first form of self-replicating life billions of years ago, the biosphere began.

Biosphere 2 lungs appear as round domes.

Biosphere 2: Laboratory for Studying How the Earth Works

Size: 3.15 acres (137,416 square feet; 12,766 square meters). The tallest point is 91 feet (28 meters) high (the rain forest roof).

Age: Completed and sealed on September 26, 1991.

Atmosphere: Biosphere 2 has 6,534,102 cubic feet (185,026 cubic meters). The "lungs" of Biosphere 2 mechanically compensate for the expansion and contraction of the air when it heats or cools inside. The two lungs are 158 feet (48 meters) in diameter, and have a maximum expansion of 1,770,546 cubic feet (50,137 cubic meters) to provide an escape for air when the atmospheric pressure changes in Biosphere 2's tightly sealed structure.

Oceans: Biosphere 2 has the largest ocean of its kind. It has nearly 1 million gallons of water made from Instant Ocean (a commercial mixture) and some natural ocean water from the Caribbean Ocean. The ocean is as deep as 25 feet (7.6 meters).

Land Mass: The soil, water, structure, and biomass estimates total 671,635 cubic feet (19,019 cubic meters).

Other: The glass surface of Biosphere 2's 6,600 panels is 170,000 square feet (15,794 square meters).

Dimensions	Square Feet N/S x E/W	Square Meters N/S x E/W	Height	
			Feet	Meters
Intensive Agricultural Area	136 x 177	41 x 54	80	24
Micro City	73 x 242	22 x 74	76	23
Rain Forest	143 x 143	44 x 44	91	28
Savannah/Ocean	275 x 100	84 x 30	87	27
Desert	121 x 121	37 x 37	75	23
Marsh	91 x 63	28 x 19	8	2
Ocean	147 x 63	45 x 19	25	8
Lungs (each)	158 x 158	48 x 48	50	15

47

The sun's energy causes water molecules to move in the biosphere in regular ways. Solar radiation causes water to evaporate from the surface of the earth (in the form of evaporation or transpiration). The evaporated water molecules condense in the troposphere's clouds. The molecules collect into droplets that form larger drops that fall in the form of precipitation. The water runs off and collects in low areas or gets down into aquifers in the ground. The process, known as the water cycle, has influenced life in many ways. The water cycle alters ecosystems, changes geological formations, and impacts other chemical cycles and processes.

OBJECTIVE: Students understand the concept of the water cycle in the biosphere.

PROCEDURE:

1. Try this combination of hands-on activity and discussion. Invite students to draw each element of the water cycle, as you draw it on the board and discuss each element.

2. Explain the concept of the water cycle with students:

The water cycle is a systematic and cyclical event that occurs in Earth's biosphere. It is systematic because the water molecules move from the planet's surface to the atmosphere and back down in very regular (systematic) ways. The water molecules move in a cycle—up and down—through the biosphere.

Evaporation and condensation.

3. Invite the student to draw each phase of the water cycle as you discuss and draw the basic water cycle which follows this process:

- **Evaporation:** The sun (the system's energy source) causes water molecules to move so fast that they change to a gaseous state—or a water vapor—and evaporate. The water vapor travels up from the surface of the oceans, lakes, rivers, and moist land areas. (The sun also causes plants to evapo-transpire—that is, to lose water from small pores in the leaves in a vapor form.)

- **Condensation:** The water vapor rises until it reaches cool air, then condenses to form clouds made of tiny water droplets. The conditions in the atmosphere must include heat, adequate air pressure, and particles in the air (for the water to cling to). In

Precipitation.

the troposphere, the air pressure and temperature become greater the closer you get to Earth's surface. The water is too heavy to condense in the thin air high in the outer layer of the atmosphere.

- **Precipitation:** The droplets come together and form larger drops that fall as precipitation—rain, snow, hail, or sleet.

- **Collection:** If the precipitation falls on land, gravity causes the water to run off the land surface and collect in streams, rivers, marshes, estuaries, lakes, oceans, glaciers, ice caps, and underground aquifers.

The water cycle is in a state of continuum in the biosphere. Earth's water supply appears in any of the four stages of the water cycle (or is stored in plants or animals and released) at one time.

Collection.

49

OBJECTIVE: Students use controlled procedures to observe the components of the water cycle.

OVERVIEW: This activity provides a simple classroom demonstration of the water cycle. The activity follows the idea that "children can embrace larger concepts after making observations and working through the thought process to connect the experience with scientific abstractions" (National Science Teachers Association, *The Content Core*). The outdoor exploration activity challenges students to apply knowledge to a framework of what they know, and describe how they know it, as a way to connect both experiences to the scientific abstraction of the water cycle.

MATERIALS NEEDED/EACH TEAM:

Bowl of hot water
(not scalding) • plastic wrap • plastic bag full of ice (small) • paper and pencil

PROCEDURE:

1. Ask students to watch and write all events inside the bowl (during the experiment) that may relate to one or all of the events of the water cycle:

Evaporation • Condensation • Precipitation • Collection

2. Instruct students to put a piece of plastic wrap over the bowl of hot water.

3. Review the students' observations, and encourage discussion of the four phases of the water cycle.

DID YOU KNOW?

Solid ice can turn into water vapor? Try freezer burn. The technical term is *sublimation*.

Assessment Suggestion

Students should be able to identify all four events of the water cycle, as well as describe how they came to those conclusions based on what they saw.

50

Biosphere 2's rain forest mountain stream.

OBJECTIVE: Students observe the natural world and its water recycling system(s).

MATERIALS NEEDED:

Notebook • pencil

PROCEDURE:

1. Challenge students to go outdoors and identify as many elements of the water cycle as possible. Recommend that they document (write and illustrate) their discoveries. Alternative: photograph or videotape the field explorations and discoveries.

2. Make it a contest. Encourage students to look for large and small evidence of the water cycle elements.

3. Invite students to present their findings aloud.

4. Extra assignment: Challenge students to identify evidence of the way(s) the water cycle has affected living or nonliving things.

Assessment Suggestion

Review the students' findings as a group. Start with the most obvious findings from your selected location, then, discuss more subtle evidence of water in its many phases of the water cycle.

51

Wet scientists. The rain forest dry down experiment started with 6,000 gallons of water cycled into the rain forest (from water reserves in Biosphere 2). Scientists then studied how the water moved through the biome.

DISCUSSION

Evaporation of water is part of the water recycling in Biosphere 2.

OBJECTIVE: Students gain a better understanding of how the water cycle works in Biosphere 2.

PROCEDURE:

1. Lead a discussion on Biosphere 2's water cycles:

Recycling: Like Earth, Biosphere 2 works with the same water that it started with. All of the water inside the enclosure is recycled. Biosphere 2 uses science and technology to create water cycles like those found in nature.

Water Supply: Ask students, *"Where is the water in Biosphere 2?"* Biosphere 2's rain forest, savannah, ocean, marsh, and desert biomes all include significant bodies of surface water. Additionally, there is moisture in the soils and water in the form of vapor in the air. The intensive agricultural biome also contains rice paddies with water several inches deep. In total, there are more than one million gallons of water sealed in Biosphere 2, with 900,000 gallons in the ocean alone.

Energy: Ask students, *"What form of energy drives the evaporation process?"* The sun. It comes through the hundreds of glass panels on Biosphere 2. The sun's light reaches the bodies of water, the plants, animals, soil, and water to promote evaporation and transpiration.

Water supply: Biosphere 2's ocean contains 900,000 gallons (3.4 million liters) of water.

Water moving in streams and collecting in a pond in Biosphere 2.

Evaporation: Ask students, *"Where does the evaporated water go in Biosphere 2?"* It goes up in Biosphere 2's atmosphere, just as it does everywhere else on Earth during the evaporation process.

Condensation: Ask students, *"Where does the water go in Biosphere 2 once it evaporates?"* The water condenses. An important part of the water cycle in Biosphere 2 is condensation. Water condenses on the inside surface of the glass panels. It condenses on the cool surfaces of the air handling system when cool air flows through the ducts.

Precipitation: Ask students, *"If water condenses on the glass panels, how does precipitation occur? And how does it rain inside Biosphere 2?"* Precipitation occurs in the form of rain in Biosphere 2. There are no clouds inside, mainly due to the air pressure. It is too low for clouds to form. Condensation runs off the glass panels to a collection system. Once collected, the water is available for distribution. A sophisticated computer-controlled "sprinkling system" simulates rainfall in Biosphere 2. Unlike Biosphere 1, computers (programmed by technicians following orders from the scientists) manage the precipitation (artificial rainfall) inside Biosphere 2.

Precipitation in Biosphere 2.

Collection and Water Usage: Not all the water collected off the glass in Biosphere 2 goes toward watering plants. Some of this water, after treatment, is used in the micro city for drinking, cooking, laundry, and cleaning uses and in the bathrooms for showers and toilets.

OBJECTIVE: Students gain an awareness of the effects of human action on the environment and the effects of the environment on humans.

MATERIALS NEEDED:

News reports on water pollution (for example stories)

PROCEDURE:

1. Invite students to bring news stories about water pollution to class, and discuss the problems with water pollution.

2. Encourage students to share the stories and comment on the environmental problem, the government policies or social issues, and the health of people who drink contaminated water, etc., depending on the story.

3. Invite students to select one of the water pollution problems apiece from the articles (their article or another student's article).

4. Invite students to write a one-page report on the human health effects of a pollutant or toxic element in the water. Students should:

- Identify the problem
- Identify the cause of the problem
- Identify the consequence of the problem
- Describe a possible solution to the problem
- Provide references used for their research

Assessment Suggestion

Students should be able to identify an example of human action that causes an environmental problem which, in turn, causes human/societal problems.

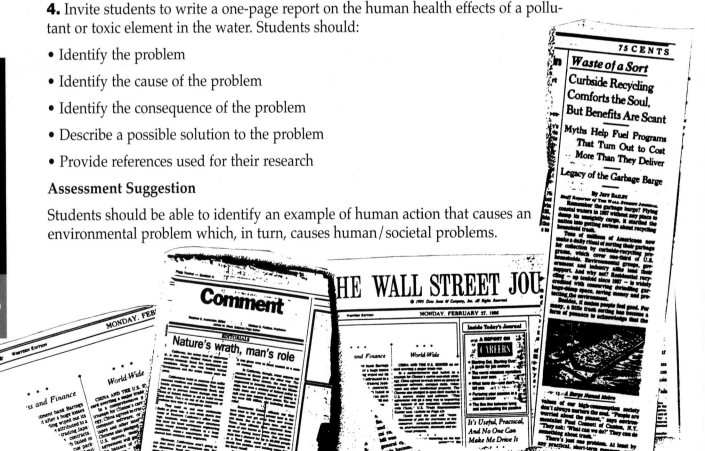

54

OBJECTIVE: Students cooperate to demonstrate and observe the effects of a human-caused problem—water pollution.

MATERIALS NEEDED:

1 clear 2-liter volume container filled with clean water • 2 tablespoons of vinegar in a small cup • 1 small bottle of red food coloring • 2 teaspoons of salt in a small cup • 2 teaspoons of coffee grounds in a small cup

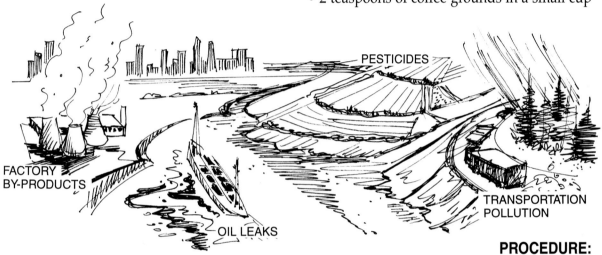

PESTICIDES

FACTORY BY-PRODUCTS

OIL LEAKS

TRANSPORTATION POLLUTION

PROCEDURE:

1. Start by having the students pass the container of clean water around the class. Ask them to imagine that the water is a clean, flowing stream.

2. Randomly distribute the vinegar, food coloring, salt, and coffee grounds to students. Pass the water around again. Ask students to add the foreign materials to the water. Ask everyone to visualize, or discuss, how this compares to how pollutants enter Earth's water supplies.

3. Invite students to think how they might process the water or control pollution if they were in Biosphere 2.

4. Lead a discussion of water and pollution, including the following information: Life uses energy to build itself into complex forms. Life has evolved to cycle and recycle materials that are available. Materials stay in the cycles for various lengths of time. Various lag times generally occur in between the time a material enters the cycle and when it completes its movement through the cycle. The problem with pollution (a form of material) is that it often does not fit into the cycle—it does not integrate. Instead, pollution often degrades or disrupts the system, the cycles, and the life systems because the living organisms are unable to pump out or respire the harmful impurities.

NOTE: Save the container with the polluted water for the next activity in which the students will "clean" the water.

55

ACTIVITY

OBJECTIVE: Students demonstrate the removal of pollutants from water using the natural phenomena of the water cycle.

MATERIALS NEEDED:

1 measuring cup (2 cup volume minimum) • 1 cup of dirty water from the first demonstration • 1 cup clean water • 1 teapot/kettle • 1 stove or hot plate (if not using an electric kettle) • 1 skillet • 12-15 ice cubes • 1 plastic bag (for ice cubes) (tie or Ziploc™) • cloth tape • 1 stirring spoon • 1 drinking cup or bowl • 2 - 4 hot pads • safety glasses, 1 per student • paper and pencil

PROCEDURE:

CAUTION: Students must use hot pads when holding the skillet over the steaming kettle. Also, safety glasses are advised.

NOTE: If you are not confident that the students can perform this experiment safely, perform it as a demonstration or have an advanced, capable group perform or assist in the demonstration.

1. Explain that this activity will demonstrate how to produce clean water.

2. Place students in teams. Challenge students to:

• Make a prediction: How will you remove the rubbish from the glass of water?

• Make observations and describe each of the following:

A. What is the energy source (heat) for your experiment?
B. Describe where the evaporation happened.
C. Describe where the condensation happened.
D. Describe where precipitation happened, and how it happened.
E. Describe where the water collected.

• **Draw a conclusion:** Did the process clean the water? Describe what happened. Try illustrating the process in the form of a diagram, such as:

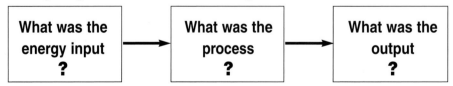

| What was the energy input ? | → | What was the process ? | → | What was the output ? |

3. Tell students to pour 1 cup of dirty water from the earlier demonstration into a 2-cup measuring cup. Then add enough clean water to make 2 cups. Stir the mixture well. Pour the mixture (entire 2 cups) into the kettle and heat it to a boil.

4. While waiting for the water to boil, have students place the ice cubes in the plastic bag and seal it. Tape the bag of ice to the bottom of the skillet. Position the empty glass (or bowl) near the kettle to catch the runoff from the skillet.

5. Tell students to hold the skillet upside down above the spout of the kettle when the water starts boiling. **Caution students not to burn themselves with the steam or the hot kettle.**

6. The water vapor will condense on the cold surface of the skillet and will fall like rain. Tell students to catch the drops of water in the glass (or bowl). Continue collecting water until there is approximately 1/2 cup of water collected in the glass.

7. Pour a little of the clear water into small cups for students who would like to taste it. Ask students: *Does it taste as if it has salt or any other element in it? Does it still look as if it has dirt or food coloring in it? Does it smell as if it has vinegar in it?* (Explain that primarily the water evaporated, condensed, precipitated, and was collected. The salt and other foreign materials should have remained in the kettle; however, sometimes volatile substances come off with boiling.)

8. Tell students to pour the remaining water into the first measuring cup. Write down the amount of water. Then add it to the amount of water collected in the other measuring cup. Ask students: *Is the total less than 2 cups? If so, where did the rest of the water go?* (Explain that the missing water went into the air in the form of water vapor.)

9. Challenge students to explain how they would get the rest of the water in their sample clean. (Solution: continue to boil it.)

10. To conclude the experiment, review the student findings.

Assessment Suggestion

Answer Key:

1. What is the energy source (heat) for your experiment? The electricity and heating unit (stove, heating element, etc.). (Note: This energy is in place of the sun.) The heat used for boiling the water represents the energy of the sun that causes water evaporation to happen in Biosphere 1 and Biosphere 2.

2. Describe the place where the evaporation happened: Through the air in the pot out to the air in the room.

3. Describe where the condensation happened: Most took place on the skillet. The rest is in the room (where some evaporated water escaped the skillet).

4. Describe where precipitation happened, and how it happened: The precipitation took place between the skillet and the container (glass or bowl). It formed drops that ran off the skillet from the force of gravity.

5. Describe where the water was collected: In the teapot and the glass or bowl. (Remember: not all of the water in the pot boiled into vapor.)

57

Waste recycling tanks in Biosphere 2 use water hyacinth and canna.

OBJECTIVE: Students gain understanding in ways to solve problems in water resource and waste water management.

PROCEDURE:

1. Lead a discussion which includes global and local issues on water quality and recycling:

• Only 3 percent of the world's water is fresh water, and most of it is frozen in the polar ice caps and glaciers. A large percentage of the remaining fresh water is not usable due to pollution. Some of this pollution comes from natural sources (bacteria, animal droppings, and other plant and animal materials), and some comes from human activities (manufacturing, electrical power generation, food processing, etc.).

• Pollution must be removed from contaminated water before we can drink it safely. Many techniques have been developed to make polluted water safe.

• Filtering is often used to take solid materials out of the water.

• Chemicals such as chlorine and hydrogen peroxide can be added to the water to kill bacteria and other microorganisms that can cause disease.

• Aeration (a process that mixes air with water) is used to increase the oxygen content of the water (added oxygen kills certain microbes). In activated sludge the oxygen is used by microbes to break down organic wastes.

• Ultraviolet light (plus hydrogen peroxide) is sometimes used to kill harmful microorganisms in the water, as is done for Biosphere 2's drinking water.

• Beneficial microbes that "eat" pollutants can be added to the water.

• Water plants such as water hyacinth and canna can be used to take some pollutants out of the water, as in Biosphere 2's recycling system.

• New technologies can be developed to prevent water pollution and to repair the damage already done. In Biosphere 2, harmful chemical pesticides and fertilizers are not allowed. Only biodegradable products that don't harm the environment are permitted. The research that is being done in Biosphere 2 is providing a greater understanding of Earth's natural recycling processes.

2. Ask students to name examples of science and technology used together to solve environmental problems.

58

OBJECTIVE: Students gain an understanding of the effect of humans on the usage of natural resources, such as water.

PROCEDURE:

1. Invite students to develop a graph that shows the relationship between water consumption and the uses of water in the United States, Mexico, the United Kingdom, and Indonesia. Use these data:

Use of Water (Percentages)			
Country	**Public Use**	**Industry**	**Agriculture**
United States	12	46	42
Mexico	6	8	86
United Kingdom	21	77	2
Indonesia	95	5	0

2. Invite students to comment on the different ways human populations use their water resources. Ask students to identify the country with the greatest balance of water usage (United States), as well as the greatest agricultural, industrial, and public use of water.

Assessment Suggestion

Students should differentiate the many ways water is used in this world, using analytical skills and graphic expressions. For example:

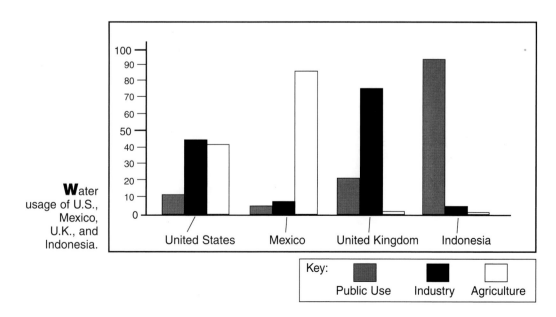

Water usage of U.S., Mexico, U.K., and Indonesia.

59

OBJECTIVE: Students gain an understanding of the cyclical nature of carbon in the biosphere.

PROCEDURE:

1. Lead a discussion with students: The circular path of chemical elements that flow back and forth between living organisms and their environment is referred to as a cycle. The biogeochemical cycles in the earth's biosphere are complex interactions between the *bios*, or living organisms, and the *ge*, or rocks, soil, air, and water of Earth. Geochemistry is a physical science focused on the chemical composition of Earth's crust, rivers, lakes, oceans, etc. Biogeochemistry is the study of the exchange of materials between the biosphere's nonliving and living things.

2. Challenge students to think about the complex biogeochemical processes in the biosphere using the carbon cycle as an example of one of many cycles that are inter-related in the biogeochemical processes on Earth.

3. Explain to students that the water cycle activities (pages 44 - 53) introduced them to the cyclical nature of elements through the biosphere. Nearly two dozen elements that provide nutrients for life cycle through the biosphere, including:

Carbon (C) • Potassium (K) • Nitrogen (N) • Phosphorus (P) • Sulfur (S)

The materials exchange at varying rates and concentrations in the biosphere. Some exchanges are slow, others fast. Their speed depends on the availability of the element and the extent of their interaction with living organisms.

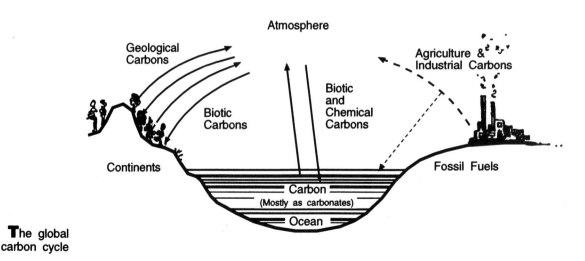

The global carbon cycle

Nearly 95 percent of all known molecules (organic and inorganic) on Earth contain the element carbon (C). Scientists say there are 4 million carbon compounds. One of the reasons for this is that carbon is one of the few elements with atoms that are able to form complicated bonds, like chains and rings. In a carbon compound, about 25-30 percent of the weight of that compound is carbon.

All plants and animals use carbon compounds to sustain life. Animals breathe in oxygen (O) and exhale carbon dioxide (CO_2). Plants take in carbon dioxide (CO_2) and release oxygen (O). Plants store the carbon in the leaves, stems, and roots. Animals eat plants (or plant eaters) and store digested carbons in their bodies. Decaying plant and animal matter gives off carbon dioxide, as does burning.

The living organisms keep the carbon cycle dynamic by processing, storing, and releasing carbon in the biosphere. In other words, carbon moves between geological sources, the living elements (biological sources), and the atmosphere. However, most of the carbon in the biosphere is exchanged between the geological and biological components of the biogeochemical cycles. Only a small percentage of total carbon in the global carbon cycle exists in the atmosphere. The most common forms are:

Carbon dioxide (CO_2) (335 ppm) • Carbon monoxide (CO) (.1 ppm) • Methane (CH_4) (1.6 ppm)

Carbon monoxide poses a threat to human health, since it reduces the oxygen-carrying capacity of the blood. Carbon monoxide concentrations in heavy automobile traffic can get as high as 100 ppm, and up to 400 ppm in the body of people who smoke a pack of cigarettes a day. High levels of methane can, among other things, disrupt the biosphere's heat balance because it is very effective at trapping infrared light.

61

DID YOU KNOW?

As a greenhouse gas, methane is estimated to be 50 times more effective at trapping heat than carbon dioxide.

OBJECTIVE: This module will help students understand that underwater ecosystems, such as coral reefs, are part of the patterns of change associated with the earth's carbon cycle.

MATERIALS NEEDED:

1 per student: copy of coral reef maps (see page 64 for master) • 1 per student: copy of common coral species (see page 65 for master) • sea shells (to show students a calcium carbonate shell)

PROCEDURE:

1. Distribute copies of the coral reef maps and the sheet of common coral species to the students.

2. Invite the students to discuss the ways carbon gets into ocean water (e.g., the motion of waves moving air into the water, materials that contain carbon dissolving into the water).

3. Provide a brief discussion of the following with the students, reading from the text or developing a similar introduction more appropriate for the group:

Coral reefs are complex communities of animals, plants, and microbes. Typically, coral reefs are located in Earth's warmest ocean areas. They occur in the warm seas of the tropics—a region that stretches around the globe from as far north as Mexico to as far south as Australia.

Animals called polyps build the coral reefs. They are relatives of sea anemones (also a polyp) and jellyfish (the medusae have a polyp stage). These creatures attach themselves to rocks near the shore and secrete calcium carbonate to build basement skeletons on which they live. When a polyp dies, its skeleton remains and new polyps use the collection of old skeletons as a base to build on. The polyp larvae — called the planula larvae — attach themselves to the structure. As the years and centuries go by, large structures grow as generation after generation of polyps build their shelters on the collection of old skeletons. A coral is a colony.

The polyps cannot build reefs all by themselves. They need the help of certain algae (zoozanthellae, a dinoflagellate), tiny photosynthetic cells that live within their bodies. In sunlight, the algae use up carbon dioxide during the photosynthesis. This process aids the coral in secreting calcium carbonate for its skeleton. The coral polyps (with the help of the algae living inside them) benefit the ocean environment by taking calcium and carbon dioxide out of the water, and transforming the material into new coral structures.

62

4. Pass around the sea shells so students can look at them and feel the hardness of the calcium carbonate. Tell students that the hardness of the shells compares to that of a hard coral. Both are made of hard materials such as calcium carbonate.

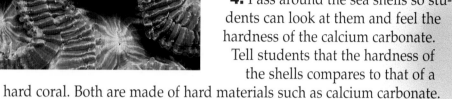

5. Invite students to look at the maps of Earth's coral reefs, and notice how many are located in shallower parts of the oceans. Compare those to the number of deep water locations.

6. Explain to students: Coral reefs can grow only in clear, nutrient-poor water. One of the reasons is that corals use sunlight to conduct photosynthesis. The algae in the coral community need the energy from sunlight to keep alive, to create hard shells for the coral polyps, and to reproduce. If the water is muddy with sediment or cloudy, not enough sunlight can get through. Even in clear water, as you go farther below the surface, less and less sunlight is available. Therefore, coral reefs are found primarily in the shallower areas of coastlines where energy can fuel the biogeochemical processes in the coral reefs. They are also found around volcanic islands away from the coasts.

7. Invite students to look at the illustrations of the common coral species while you discuss the next subject.

8. Explain to students: The varieties of coral number in the hundreds, and each has a building pattern of its own. The pattern is determined by the type of food the polyp eats and the flow of the sea water that carries the food to it. Some, like the brain coral, build their skeletons side by side, then layer upon layer, making a smooth, rounded structure. Others, like the sea fan, form in the shape of flat, lacy branches. Some look like umbrellas, flowers, trees, or fingers. The coral reef communities build hard calcium carbonate structures, thus storing carbon in their underwater world.

63

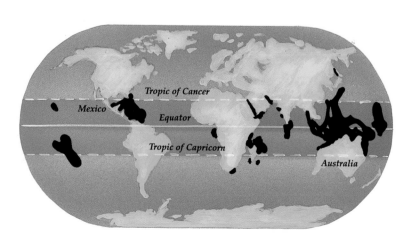

Coral Reefs
of the World.

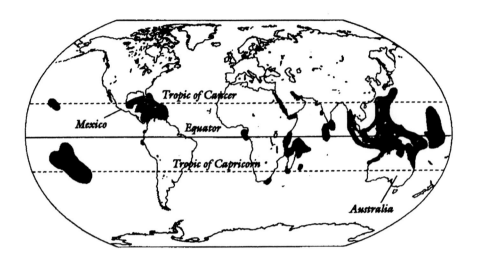

EARTH'S CORAL REEFS (ESTIMATED)

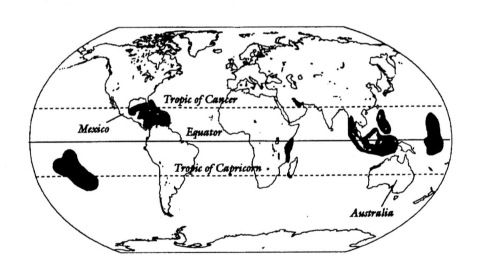

CORAL REEFS THAT ARE CONSIDERED ENDANGERED (ESTIMATED)

64

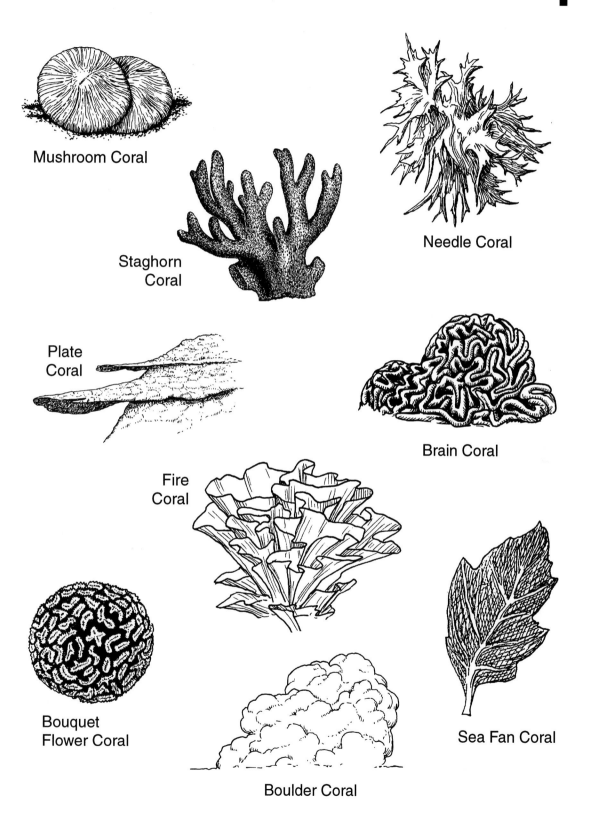

Mushroom Coral

Staghorn Coral

Needle Coral

Plate Coral

Brain Coral

Fire Coral

Bouquet Flower Coral

Boulder Coral

Sea Fan Coral

65

Ocean life in
Biosphere 2.

9. Explain a few of the issues related to the coral reefs and global ecology: Throughout Earth's history coral reefs have served many purposes. They protect shorelines by minimizing waves as they approach land. They control the levels of minerals that drain from land into the ocean.

Coral reefs are home to a great diversity of ocean creatures that are dependent on the food web and shelter provided in the reefs. Coral reefs play a major part in recycling gases in the atmosphere:

• Corals take carbon dioxide from ocean water, allowing the oceans to absorb more carbon dioxide from the atmosphere. Corals use the carbon from carbon dioxide as a building block for skeleton building.

• The algae that live in the coral give off a great deal of oxygen in the process of photosynthesis.

Research tells us that reefs can grow only in certain sets of conditions. The water must be warm, but not too warm. At higher temperatures, coral can "bleach" and lose the much needed zooxanthallae (the algae in this symbiotic relationship). The water must have salt in it, but not too much and not too little. The water must be within a certain pH range—not too acid and not too alkaline—about 8.2 to 8.4 on a scale of 0 to 14. The water must have a low nutrient content. Nutrients, such as nitrates and phosphates, lead to an overgrowth of plankton. When plankton build up they block out sunlight, thus choking off the corals. For growth, corals need cadmium, strontium, and iodine, too.

A marine scientist conducts research in Biosphere 2's ocean.

Thousands of species of animals live in and around Earth's coral reefs. If a coral reef is damaged in any way, all of these other creatures are damaged or destroyed as well. Many of the dangers to coral reefs are human-caused. Fishing is a major problem. In some parts of the world fishing crews use dynamite to stun the fish to make them easy to catch. The explosions often shatter or crush the coral structures. Other fishing crews drag nets through the water to catch fish, and the nets break off parts of the coral and scar the reefs.

Tourists can be harmful to reefs. Boats traveling above reefs break off parts of the coral as they pass, and divers often collect pieces of coral to take home with them as souvenirs.

Reefs are sometimes destroyed by heavy machinery, either for use as building materials or to extend the land area along the shore.

When the nearby land is cleared for farming, rain washes soil into the ocean. The sediments in the water can either smother the coral community or cloud the water so that not enough sunlight can get through to keep the coral alive and growing.

Trash, oil, and chemicals in the water are also hazardous to corals. Another danger is hot water. Nuclear plants and some factories use large amounts of water to cool the machinery. They can release very hot water into the ocean.

Through research, scientists can begin to understand how to restore the damaged coral reefs. People can help coral reef protection and research by supporting the work of research organizations or by promoting awareness in their community, writing letters to government representatives and businesses, etc.

10. Assemble students into teams of four to six. Invite students to reflect on the discussion and prepare a presentation or position paper, to address both of the following:

• How do the locations of coral reefs relate to water temperatures (is there an energy factor)?

• How do the locations of coral reefs relate to water depths?

Life in Biosphere 2 ocean takes many shapes.

67

CAUTION

The temperature of dry ice is -110°F (-70°C) or lower. If your bare skin touches it, even for an instant, its extreme cold can cause serious, permanent skin damage.

OBJECTIVE: This section is designed to show how calcium carbonate is formed so students can correlate the phenomenon to shells and coral reefs.

MATERIALS NEEDED:

2 large clear glass jars (2 quarts minimum) • 1 pair heavy insulated gloves • 1 pair tongs • 1 quart water for lime water mixture • 3 cups water for demonstration • 1 sticky label and pen • 1 tbsp. lime • 1 chunk dry ice about half the size of a deck of playing cards (2" x 2" x 1") or several smaller chunks (dry ice can be obtained at ice cream stores and some large supermarkets) • 1 seashell

PROCEDURE:

NOTE: Keep samples of both the carbonic acid and calcium carbonate (made during this activity) for use in the activity described on page 71: *Phenomenal pH.*

1. Prepare a one-quart mixture of lime water several hours before class:

• Add one tablespoon of lime (mineral) to a quart of water in a wide-mouthed juice bottle. (You can get lime at a building supply store.)

• Put the cap on the bottle and shake well. Allow the lime to settle to the bottom of the bottle. This may take several hours.

• Carefully pour off some of the clear lime water from the top into a jar with a tight cover. Label the jar "Lime water."

2. Explain to the students that carbonic acid is formed when the dry ice reacts with the water as you perform the demonstration. Carbon dioxide is one of the most water soluble gases in the atmosphere.

• Pour three cups of water into the glass container.

• Put on the gloves to protect your hands. Use the tongs to put the dry ice into the water. Explain to the students that dry ice is solid carbon dioxide. It will react with the water by producing gas (bubbles) and altering the water's composition.

• After the bubbling stops, the cup or jar will contain a weak acid called carbonic acid, also found in soda pop. Label the jar "Carbonic acid."

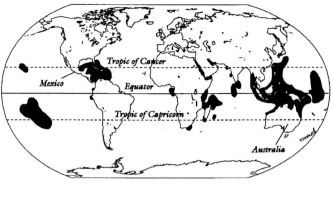

The world's coral reefs.

3. Explain to the students that lime contains calcium, and that the clear lime water has calcium in it. Pour about 2 cups of lime water into the other container. Add about 2 cups of the clear carbonic acid solution to the lime water. Ask the students to describe what they think they are seeing.

NOTE: Hold up the shell and the container with calcium carbonate.

4. Explain to students that when the clear carbonic acid comes together with the clear lime water, a white precipitate called calcium carbonate will form. The precipitate is caused by putting lime in an acidic solution.

This is the same material that makes up the skeletons of corals and other ocean creatures.

The sea animals bring together carbon dioxide and calcium from ocean water to form their calcium carbonate shells.

5. Explain to the students that the demonstration shows a chemical process similar to one used by living animals. The carbon compound, such as calcium carbonate, contains carbon, oxygen, and a metal—that's where the limestone came in.

As mentioned on pages 60 and 61, there is an interdependence and relationship between the living organisms and their immediate physical, chemical, and biological environment.

The carbon compound, such as calcium carbonate, contains carbon and oxygen (from the carbon dioxide and water), and another source of carbon from the limestone.

69

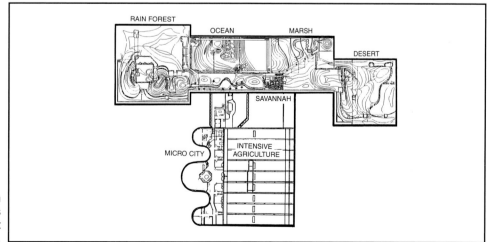

Carbon is stored in living systems throughout Biosphere 2.

The Biosphere 2 ocean, above and below, has many biogeochemical interactions that occur day and night.

6. Ask students to:

• Describe the similarity between this demonstration and the relationship of the coral producing its shell.

• Describe what they think would happen if the water were polluted. Could the calcium carbonate form the same way?

Suggested Assessment

Students should be able to articulate that:

• There is a chemical process that takes place in water.

• The process, in the case of the coral reef, illustrates one of the biogeochemical cycles: the carbon cycle.

• The coral reefs might not be productive in polluted water, since the animals that form the reefs (corals) favor nutrient poor environments (opposed to the algae that overgrow the corals which favor high nutrient levels).

OBJECTIVE: Students perform pH tests and correlate those tests to uses in scientific research, including coral reef studies where the carbon cycle affects pH.

MATERIALS NEEDED/EACH TEAM:

1 per student: pH Data Sheets (see page 72) • 1 per student: pen or pencil • 1 measuring cup • 1 teaspoon • 5 clear glass jars • 5 sticky labels • 6 strips of blue litmus paper (or other pH-testing device) • 6 strips of red litmus paper (or other pH-testing device) • 1/4 cup calcium carbonate solution from the earlier experiment • 1/4 cup lime water from earlier experiment • 1/4 cup carbonic acid from the earlier experiment • 1/4 cup water • 1 tsp. vinegar • 1 tsp. baking soda • 5 stirring spoons or sticks

NOTES ON MATERIALS: Litmus paper is only one of many ways to check the pH of a liquid. The options are simple or complex, from pH test kits you can get in a hardware or swimming pool supply store to advanced technologies and instruments used by professionals.

Options: If you cannot acquire litmus paper or pH testing equipment, it is easy to make your own test strips. In a few minutes you can boil red cabbage, then pour off the purple liquid. Cut coffee filters into strips and dip them into the liquid. Let the strips dry. (During the test, the strip turns blue when dipped in a liquid that is a base. It turns pink if the liquid is an acid.)

Amounts: If you decide to use kits, you need six pH test kits for the six samples the students will measure. If you make your own paper, each team of students will need six strips to complete the experiments.

71

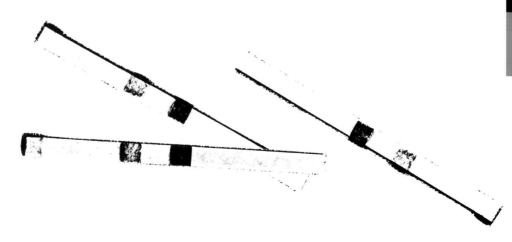

Other interesting pH factors:

Acid rain: 3

Cola: 3.1 - 3.3

Rain water: 5.5

Saliva: 6.24

Blood: 7.41

Laundry detergents: 13

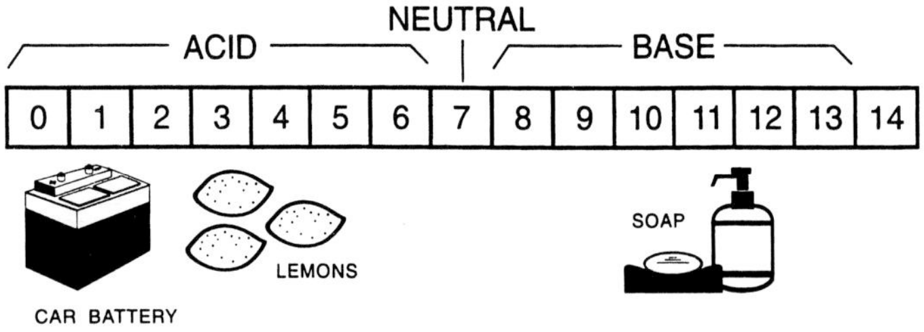

```
        NEUTRAL
/--- ACID ---\  |  /------ BASE ------\
| 0 | 1 | 2 | 3 | 4 | 5 | 6 | 7 | 8 | 9 | 10 | 11 | 12 | 13 | 14 |
```

CAR BATTERY   LEMONS   SOAP

pH DATA SHEET

	Acid	Base	Neutral
Jar **A** (baking soda)			
Jar **B** (vinegar)			
Jar **C** (carbonic acid)			
Jar **D** (limewater)			
Jar **E** (calcium carbonate solution, before vinegar)			
Jar **E** (calcium carbonate solution after vinegar)			
Test these solutions and check (✓) whether they are acid, base or neutral			

72

PROCEDURE:

1. Organize the students into teams.

2. Distribute and review the pH Data Sheets with students. The pH scale is used in science to measure how acidic or alkaline (basic) a liquid is. The term "pH" stands for "potential for hydrogen." The pH scale is a negative log of the hydrogen ion concentration. The higher the number is on the pH scale, the lower the hydrogen (H^+) concentration and the greater the hydroxide (OH) concentration in the water (H_2O). (The hydrogen ion is a free proton (+) charge without an electron.)

An acid is a substance that donates hydrogen ions in a chemical reaction. An acid is a chemical compound that contains hydrogen and at least one other element. Acids are usually liquid. Strong acids can burn skin, and even dissolve metals. Hydrochloric acid (HCl) is a strong acid. Hydrochloric acid is found in the body's gastric juices. It helps digest food in the stomach.

A base solution accepts hydrogen ions in a chemical reaction. A base is the product of a chemical reaction with oxygen or hydrogen. A base reacts with an acid to form a compound of salt plus water, which "neutralize" each other.

The numbers on the pH scale start at 0 and go up to 14. The most acidic solution is rated 0. The most alkaline (basic) solution is rated 14. This is a scale based on powers of ten. Because the scale's logarithm is inverse, or negative, a substance with a pH of 2 is ten times less acidic than a substance with a pH of 1 on the pH scale.

3. Explain that scientists, environmentalists, and agronomists study pH levels in soils and water to be able to manage the health of animals and plants in a biome. Ask the class to discuss why they think that might be important.

4. Explain to students that they will use chemistry to test the pH levels of solutions. The tool they will use is litmus paper, and the litmus paper shows whether a liquid is an acid or base. (More sophisticated testing paper or equipment is available that shows variations in pH.) Litmus paper has absorbed a chemical (water-soluble anthrocyanin) from red cabbage which reacts by changing color.

73

5. Lead students through the set-up for the experiment. When all teams have finished with jar A, have them go on to jar B, etc., as follows:

• Pour a few ounces of water into a jar.
Add about a teaspoonful of baking soda and stir it well. Label the jar A.

• Pour a few ounces of vinegar into a jar. Label the jar B.

• Pour some carbonic acid (previously mixed, see pg. 68) into a jar, and label it C.

• Pour some lime water (previously mixed, see p. 68) into a jar, and label it D.

• Pour calcium carbonate solution (previously mixed, see p. 68) into a jar, and label it E.

6. Instruct the students to use the litmus paper (or other test) to test the pH levels of the liquids in all of the jars. Invite them to write the results (acid, base, or neutral) on the pH Data Sheet. Tell students:

• If blue litmus paper turns red or pink when it is dipped into a liquid, it means that the liquid is an acid (pH between 0 and 7).

• If red litmus paper turns blue when it is dipped into a liquid, it means that the liquid is a base (pH between 7 and 14).

74

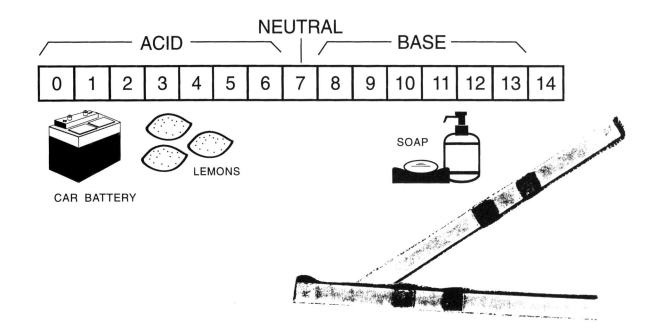

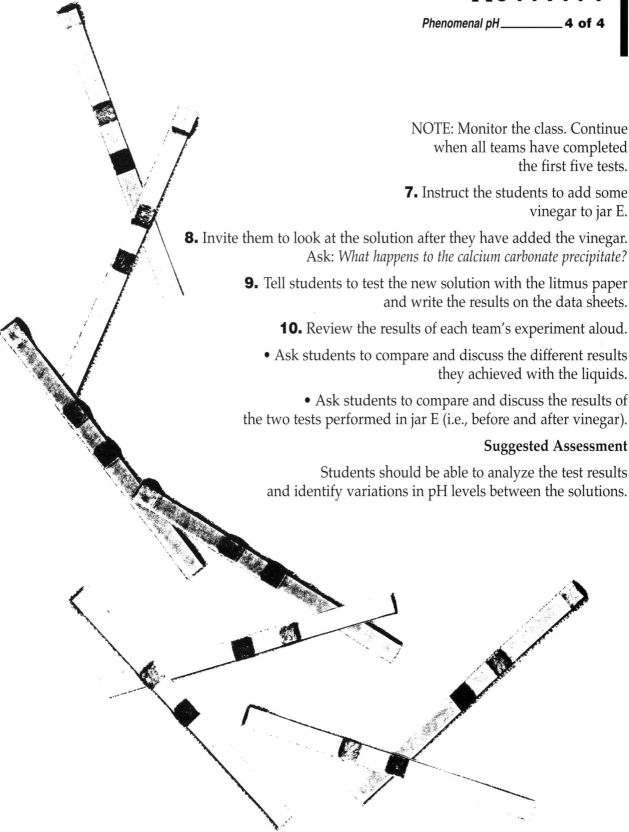

NOTE: Monitor the class. Continue when all teams have completed the first five tests.

7. Instruct the students to add some vinegar to jar E.

8. Invite them to look at the solution after they have added the vinegar. Ask: *What happens to the calcium carbonate precipitate?*

9. Tell students to test the new solution with the litmus paper and write the results on the data sheets.

10. Review the results of each team's experiment aloud.

• Ask students to compare and discuss the different results they achieved with the liquids.

• Ask students to compare and discuss the results of the two tests performed in jar E (i.e., before and after vinegar).

Suggested Assessment

Students should be able to analyze the test results and identify variations in pH levels between the solutions.

75

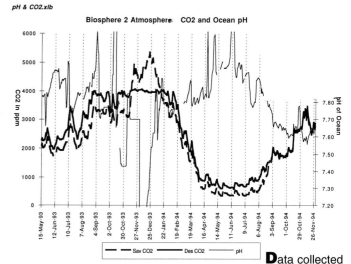

pH & CO2.xlb

Biosphere 2 Atmospheric CO2 and Ocean pH

Data collected from Biosphere 2 indicates a relationship between carbon dioxide and ocean pH.

OBJECTIVE: Students, through the use of technology, can see how changes in the environment can have a cause-and-effect relationship with other factors in the environment.

MATERIALS NEEDED:

1 per student: copy of Biosphere 2 Data with the Atmospheric CO_2 & Ocean pH Levels chart and Atmospheric CO_2 & External Total Quantum Light chart (see page 77) (or make overhead transparencies, and use with an overhead projector).

PROCEDURE:

1. Distribute copies of the Atmospheric CO_2 and Ocean pH chart and the Atmospheric CO_2 and External Total Quantum Light chart to the students.

2. Explain that the data in the chart was acquired from Biosphere 2 sensing and computing systems. Point out the quantum light line and the pH line on the chart. Ask students to draw a conclusion about the relationship between the atmospheric carbon dioxide (CO_2) levels, the light levels, and the pH levels in the Biosphere 2 ocean.

3. Explain that the chart shows Biosphere 2 atmospheric carbon dioxide and ocean biome pH levels. The greatest differences can be seen from February 1994 through October 1994. A relationship between atmospheric carbon dioxide and pH level is visible. The higher the carbon dioxide level goes, the lower the pH seems to go. The lower the carbon dioxide level appears, the higher the pH seems to appear. Coral reefs of the world's oceans have a pH of 8.2 to 8.4. The coral reef community of the Biosphere 2 ocean has tolerated lower pH levels and been able to stay healthy.

76

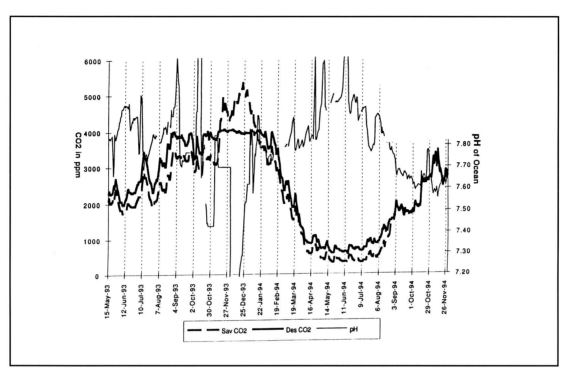

BIOSPHERE 2 OCEAN pH & CO$_2$ DATA

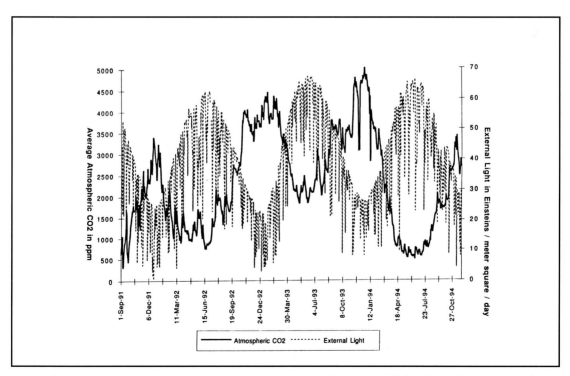

BIOSPHERE 2 EXTERNAL QUANTUM LIGHT & ATMOSPHERIC CO$_2$ DATA

Biosphere 2 computers process many types of data.

4. Review the levels of Biosphere 2 atmospheric carbon dioxide and external quantum light. Note the correlation between low light levels and higher carbon dioxide output. Higher light levels correlate to lower carbon dioxide in the atmosphere, largely due to the increased uptake of carbon dioxide during the photosynthetic process when the photosynthetic rate exceeds the respiration rate. Carbon dioxide in the atmosphere dissolves in water as a gas.

5. Invite students to discuss the reasons for the rise, fall, and crossover of the atmospheric CO_2 line in relationship to the rise, fall, and crossover of the external light line in the chart.

6. Invite students to compare the carbon dioxide readings in this chart from April through July, to the carbon dioxide levels in the chart on page 77.

7. Compare the light levels and pH levels.

8. Ask students to discuss why they think there is or is not a relationship between light, pH, and carbon dioxide levels.

DID YOU KNOW?

When carbon dioxide is combined with water, carbonic acid (H_2CO_3) is formed. This can alter into a bicarbonate (HCO_3) and then to a carbonate (CO_3). Only the dissolved carbon dioxide gas and HCO_3 (bicarbonate) are used by algae (plants) in photosynthesis. (The CO_3 can combine with the calcium to form lime: $CaCO^3$).

Suggested Assessment

Students should be able to interpret the Biosphere 2 charts and identify a correlation between the energy source (light), the carbon cycle (carbon dioxide changes), and a chemical characteristic (pH) inside Biosphere 2.

OBJECTIVE: Students gain an understanding of how microorganisms are linked to the delicate balance of life and the biogeochemical processes in the biosphere.

MATERIALS NEEDED/EACH TEAM:

1 instruction & data sheet (see page 80) • 4 quart-size Ziploc™ bags • 4 packets of activated dry yeast • 2 tsp. sugar • 1 measuring spoon (teaspoon) • 1 measuring cup • 6 cups warm water • 1 large bowl • 1 marking pen(permanent ink) • 1 thermometer • 1 tablet of paper with a stiff back • 1 ruler • 1 pen or pencil

PROCEDURE:

1. Tell the students that in this module they will learn about the role of microorganisms and some of the ways they function in terms of the biogeochemical cycles in the biosphere.

2. Explain: The organisms used in this experiment are in the dry form (dormant) and must have water in order to become activated. Many scientists are interested in the effects of natural recycling that takes place in the earth's biosphere. Recycling biodegradable material often requires the presence of moisture for the microorganisms (the creatures responsible for the biological breakdown of trash) to be activated.

3. Explain: The yeast consists of living organisms (biological components of the experiment) and will breakdown (decompose) the substrate (sugar and water) and respire to produce carbon dioxide. Scientists often study the smallest of creatures in synthesizing data about the planet's biosphere.

Yeast organisms produce carbon dioxide gas like many of the microorganisms in Biosphere 2. Carbon dioxide is an atmospheric gas that requires strict monitoring by computers that receive information from CO$_2$ sensors each day in Biosphere 2. If the carbon dioxide level gets too high, technologists can use specialized equipment, such as a CO$_2$ scrubber, to reduce it. The scrubber extracts the CO$_2$ from the atmosphere.

4. Ask students to write a brief description of how the yeast used in this experiment might be connected to the life cycles, the water cycles, and the carbon cycles in the biosphere.

• After the experiment, ask students to review their descriptions.

• Explore how their descriptions or interpretations of the connections change after the experiment.

5. Explain to students that it is hard to see a microbe without a microscope. Add that people can see evidence of microbes "eating," which is how they break down sources of food (in this case sugar) that provide energy for their tiny systems. In this way, microorganisms help recycle materials. One of the byproducts of this decomposing activity is the release of carbon dioxide into the atmosphere.

Continued on page 81

1. Pour one packet of activated dry yeast into each of the four Ziploc™ bags.

2. Add 1 teaspoon of sugar to one of the bags and write 1 t on the outside of the bag with the marking pen.

3. Add 1/2 teaspoon of sugar to another bag and mark 1/2 t on the bag.

4. Add 1/4 teaspoon of sugar to the fourth bag and mark 1/4 t on the bag.

5. Mark 0 on the outside of the last bag and do not add any sugar to it.

6. Pour warm water into the large bowl so that it is about 2/3 full. Check the temperature of the water with the thermometer. The water should be about 115 degrees F (46 degrees C). Add hot or cold water to bring the water to this temperature.

7. Use the measuring cup to dip 1/4 cup of warm water from the bowl into each of the bags. Gently squeeze each bag between your fingers to mix the contents thoroughly. Make sure that there are no dry pockets of yeast or sugar in the bags.

8. Squeeze most of the air out of the bags and seal them. Set the bags in the bowl of warm water in a warm place so it will not cool down rapidly. Wait 30 to 40 minutes.

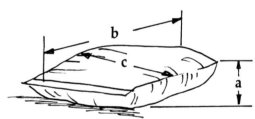

80

DATA SHEET

Bag	Distance from table to bottom of tablet (inches) (a)	Length of bag (inches) (b)	Width of bag (inches) (c)	Approximate volume of carbon dioxide in bag (cubic inches) (a x b x c)
0				
1/4 t				
1/2 t				
1t				

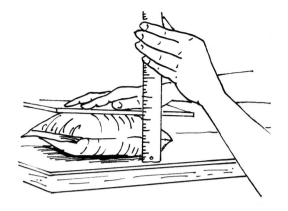

6. Organize the students into teams. Distribute materials and instruction sheets to the teams.

7. Instruct the students to set up the experiment; encourage them to follow the instructions closely.

8. When the students finish, note the time. Allow 30 to 40 minutes for the yeast to produce adequate levels of carbon dioxide for students to analyze easily.

NOTE: Do not open any of the bags until all measurements have been taken.

9. Remind the students that the yeast organisms produced carbon dioxide in the process of decomposing their food (the sugar). The carbon dioxide is captured in the bag.

10. Tell the students to:

• Take the bag marked 0 out of the water, dry it, and place it on a flat table.

• Put the tablet of paper on top of the bag, holding the tablet in a level position.

• Use the ruler to measure the distance from the table to the bottom of the tablet.

• Record the measurements on the data sheet.

• Repeat this procedure with the bags marked 1/4 t, 1/2 t, and 1 t.

11. Have the students calculate the approximate volume of carbon dioxide in each of the bags by following the procedure shown on the data sheet.

CO$_2$ trivia:
Bakers use the yeast organisms in many types of bread to make the texture lighter and fluffier. The organisms do this by consuming some of the ingredients in the dough, including sugar. The carbon dioxide forms bubbles in the dough. These are the holes in the finished bread.

DID YOU KNOW?

That yeast organisms take in sugar (a form of plant material) through their cell walls and membranes? They have no mouths!

81

12. Encourage students to summarize the results of their experiments and correlate the investigations to the carbon cycle, the water cycle, and the biological component of the earth's biosphere.

Ask students to describe their calculations. Compare the measurements each group found with 0, 1/4 t, 1/2 t, and 1 t bags.

Ask the teams to explain why some of the bags expanded more than others, and how they know what they know about the changes in the bags.

13. Explain again that the plastic bags now contain various amounts of carbon dioxide in the gaseous form.

• The yeast organisms produced this gas when they decomposed their food (the sugar).

• There are different amounts of gas in the bags because more decomposition took place in the bags with larger amounts of sugar.

• The bag that had no sugar in it has no new carbon dioxide in it at all.

Biosphere 2 waste recycling systems use aerobic (left) and anaerobic (right, white tanks) microorganisms.

14. Ask students how they think this experiment relates to the biogeochemical cycles in Earth's biosphere, especially how the water cycle, the carbon cycle, and the biological forces interact.

Suggested Assessment

Students should be able to articulate essential elements of the experiment, including the fact that microorganisms are significant to the decomposition of materials in the biosphere. Students should also identify the connection between the living organisms and atmospheric CO_2 in the biosphere.

OBJECTIVE: To increase students' awareness of the effect of the energy source, elements of the carbon cycle, elements of the water cycle, and functions of the microorganisms in biogeochemical processes in the biosphere.

MATERIALS NEEDED:

Paper • Pen/Pencil

PROCEDURE:

1. Lead a discussion on some of the roles of microorganisms in the biogeochemical processes of the biosphere. Explain to students that among the cycles in the biosphere, there are two major groups:

The physical samples are analyzed in Biosphere 2's Analytics Laboratory.

- Gaseous cycles (mostly in the atmosphere)

- Sedimentary cycles (mostly in the soils and sediments in the earth's crust as calcium carbonate)

The global carbon cycle includes forms of carbon compounds in both groups. Carbon can be found in:

- The atmosphere (such as carbon dioxide and carbon monoxide)

- The terrestrial areas (in biomass, fossil fuels, and sediments)

- Oceans (in coral reefs, for example)

NOTE: Nitrogen, sometimes found in the soil, is primarily in the atmosphere. Phosphorus is primarily in Earth's soils.

In the previous experiment, the yeast—one of thousands of forms of microorganisms—demonstrated the ability of tiny living systems to break down foods for energy. The presence of air and water was required. The water brought the yeast out of dormancy. The yeast used oxygen and sugar, and respired carbon dioxide. The conditions inside Biosphere 2 are optimal for microorganisms. It is warm and moist. An abundance of food can be found in the form of animal waste and plant litter. Recycling and composting have to be managed closely because the microorganisms can upset the balance of atmospheric gases inside Biosphere 2 within hours.

83

In the experiment, you saw that, when the yeast organisms are in a moist environment that provides the right temperature and the right kind of food, they are able to be activated from their dormant form and begin to convert oxygen and sugar into carbon dioxide.

It is important to note that if it is too hot, the yeast organisms will die. If it is too cool during the experiment, the decomposition process will take much longer. (This is why we keep many of our foods in the refrigerator—to delay their decomposition by microbes.) If it were too cold, the yeast microorganisms would not become active at all.

2. Draw the BIO 2 Carbon Dioxide chart (below) on a board for the students to study. Explain to the students that the chart shows the relationship between the sun's energy and the carbon cycle where microorganisms are involved.

3. Challenge students to explain the carbon dioxide level increase from January to February. For example, the sun's energy coming into the biosphere (in the chart) is similar to the heat from the water in the yeast experiments. Does the sun level increase from a cloudy January to a sunny February affect carbon dioxide?

Suggested Assessment

Students should be able to explain the effect of the energy source, on the biological and chemical processes.

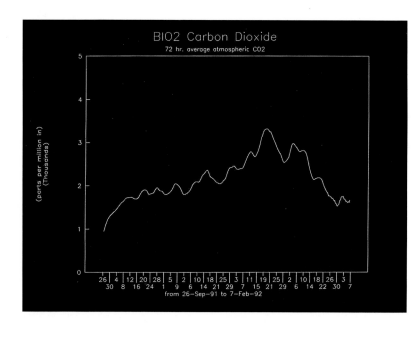

Checking the carbon dioxide: The ratio of atmosphere-to-soil in Biosphere 2 is small (compared to that in Biosphere 1 with its thick atmosphere above the thin soil layer). The microorganisms' respiration can quickly increase carbon dioxide levels in the Biosphere 2 atmosphere. The smaller atmosphere also has a far greater daily surge (up to 700 parts per million) of carbon dioxide than the 1 or 2 parts per million in Earth's atmosphere. Technologists and scientists monitor carbon dioxide levels in Biosphere 2 using sensors and computers. Every fifteen minutes, a new value for carbon dioxide appears on the "global monitor" computer screen in Biosphere 2's Biospheric Operations. This information comes from the sensors distributed throughout Biosphere 2.

84

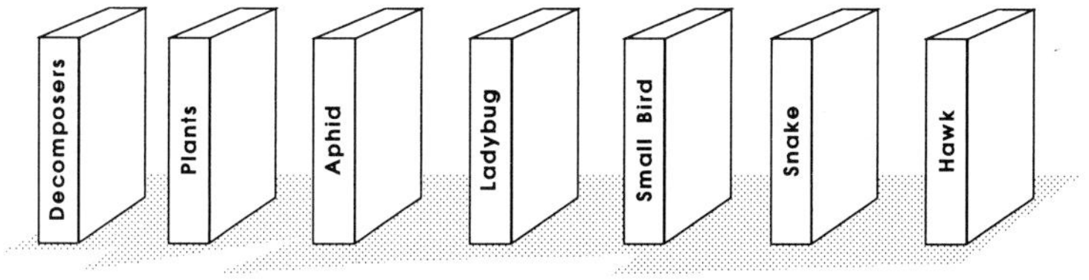

Decomposers | Plants | Aphid | Ladybug | Small Bird | Snake | Hawk

OBJECTIVE: Students gain an awareness of the role of microorganisms in the food chain and the relationship of the food chain (and food web) to the biogeochemical processes in the biosphere.

MATERIALS NEEDED:

7 pictures of food chain members (see pages 87 to 94) glued onto 7 cereal boxes (or equivalent)

PROCEDURE:

1. Prepare this demonstration on food chains & microbes in advance of the class:

- To demonstrate how a food chain works, set up a display, using cereal boxes representing the various parts of a food chain.

- Make sure that the boxes are placed so that if you push on the Decomposers box the rest will fall like dominoes, and if you remove any box from the row, the boxes beyond that one will remain standing when you push the Decomposers box over.

- Push the Decomposers box over. This demonstration is fun when students get involved in the domino action. Have an assistant help.

2. Develop a discussion for students to explain that:

There is a world so very small that we need the powers of technology to enable our eyes to see its diversity and activities. In this world live the essential microorganisms. They are necessary for our biogeochemical processes to operate as they do to sustain larger life in the biosphere. From the oceans to the mountain tops, microorganisms of all shapes and sizes participate in the biological, geological, and chemical interactions in the biosphere. Earth's microorganisms are purposeful and alive in a form barely visible—and often invisible—to the naked eye. The microorganisms are producers and decomposers. They respire, eat other microorganisms, and multiply, too. They are square one of any food chain and food web. For example, marine animals depend on blue-green algae (now called cyanobacteria), especially smaller fish . . . that are food for larger fish . . . which are food for even larger fish. This chain of feeding events is known as a simple food chain.

Microorganisms—such as fungi, molds, and bacteria—play an important part in natural food chains by decomposing plant and animal material so that the nutrients contained in them are made available for new plants to grow.

Each box represents a link in the food chain. The action of the falling boxes symbolizes one animal receiving food from the preceding member of the food chain. When all of the boxes have fallen, it means that all of the links (members) have connected (eaten) and will survive. If a box remains standing, it means that a link of the food chain has not connected (eaten) its food source and is in danger of dying.

85

3. Show students how the missing link in the food chain works by removing the Ladybug box from the row. Make sure the boxes are spaced so that the Aphid box will not touch the Bird box when it falls. Push the Decomposers box over. The Bird, Snake, and Hawk boxes will still be standing. This activity shows students that without some members of the food chain, other members of the food chain could be in danger of extinction.

4. Show students how important the microorganisms are in the food chain. Line up all of the boxes again, and remove the Decomposers box. "Push" the empty space where the Decomposers box had been, and point out that without the decomposers none of the other food chain links can survive.

Ladybugs are used in Biosphere 2's biological pest management program.

5. Explain that Biosphere 2 depends on microorganisms in its food chain to decompose materials. Besides producing food for plants, they are recyclers of dead plants, materials, and wastes.

6. Explain that a food web is a more complicated model of the connection between living things and their food sources. For example, the bird may eat the ladybug, as well as a variety of other insects, plant seeds, and other things found in the biosphere. Food sources for the bird may be food sources for other species that live in the same habitat as the bird. A mouse may eat the same type of seed the bird eats, for example.

7. Challenge students to draw an example of a food web. A pond-based food web with a kingfisher or other keystone predator provides a variety of living organisms students can easily draw upon previous knowledge to construct a food web schematic.

86

DID YOU KNOW?

Some bacteria can decompose at very low temperatures, even in the freezer? That's why ice cream can spoil.

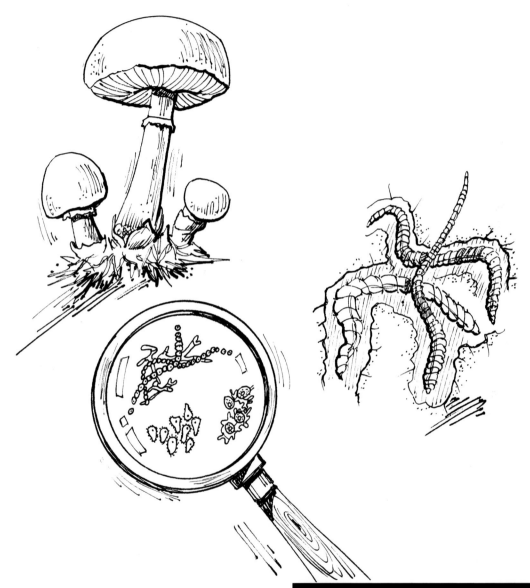

87

DID YOU KNOW?

Some decomposers eat other decomposers?

88

DID YOU KNOW?

Some plants, like the Venus flytrap, eat insects?

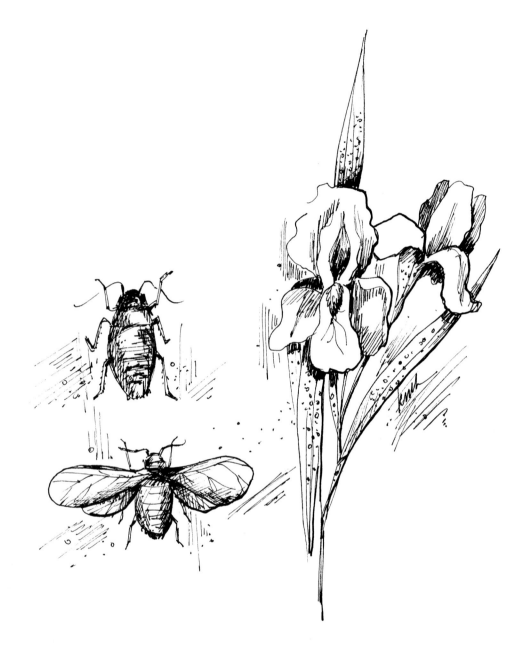

89

DID YOU KNOW?

Aphids drink plant sap with a stylet? It's a kind of ectoparasite.

90

DID YOU KNOW?

Ladybugs are used to control aphids in gardens, in place of chemical pesticides?

91

DID YOU
KNOW?

Sparrows and all birds have two stomachs. The sparrow eats insects as well as seeds and other plant produce.

92

DID YOU KNOW?

Young birds and eggs are food for many types of snakes all over the world?

DID YOU KNOW?

The shape of a bird's bill shows the type of food the bird eats. Hooked bills, like this hawk's bill, are designed to tear flesh.

93

OBJECTIVE:

Students cooperate with each other outside of the classroom to look for evidence of microbial activity and to document their findings.

MATERIALS NEEDED:

1 notebook • 1 large spoon or small shovel • 1 pen or pencil • 1 plastic bag for collecting samples • 1 magnifying glass (optional) • 1 camera (optional)

PROCEDURE:

1. Organize the students into small teams and distribute the bags and other tools for collecting samples/data.

2. Explain that this activity takes place outdoors. Students should look for and document examples of natural decomposition of organic materials by microbes.

3. Tell students to document, draw, or photograph their findings and to:

• Look for mushrooms or other types of fungi. These grow by feeding on dead organic material.

• Look for dead leaves under trees and other plants. Pick some up and look at them. Leaves may have mold growing on their surfaces. Some leaves may have parts missing, which can be an indication that material has already been decomposed and has become part of the soil. Students should collect samples of decomposing leaves in the plastic bags.

• Try to find a rotting log or tree branch. Look at it carefully using the magnifying glass.

• Dig up a small sample of the soil under a plant or bush. Examine it with your magnifying glass. You may see earthworms, insects and other creatures. Look for tiny strands of mold fibers in the soil.

• Moist places are good places to find microbes. Check under a rock. Do it carefully—you may surprise an unfriendly creature.

• You may see bodies of dead creatures (insects, worms, spiders, and animals). Don't touch them. They may carry harmful microorganisms. Dead animals can have live fleas and ticks around them.

4. Allow at least 10 to 20 minutes for students to explore the outdoors for microbial evidence.

5. Return to the classroom and have each team share its findings.

6. Optional: Create a research wall. Allow students to place their drawings and photographs on a wall in the classroom. Invite students to review each other's documentation.

Field notes are an important part of data collection inside Biosphere 2. Here, a Biospherian documents observations in the rain forest.

Suggested Assessment

Students should be able to identify evidence of the decomposition of natural materials, and document their findings (using written descriptions, drawings, photographs, or other methods of documentation).

95

Sample Field Research Data Sheet Format

Date: _____

Time: _____

Field Research _____

Evidence of Microbial Activity _____

Ecosystem (Forest, field, desert, rotting log, rock, etc.)	Evidence of Decomposition	Organisms (leaves, dead animals, insects, worms, fungus, etc.)

Components of the Atmosphere

The atmosphere of Earth is divided into the atmospheric layers: the troposphere, the stratosphere (where the ozone layer is found), the mesosphere, the thermosphere, the ionosphere (charged particles in the thermosphere), and the exosphere. Many people take for granted the fact that the gases in Earth's atmosphere stay near the planet. What keeps all of the oxygen, carbon dioxide, hydrogen, and other types of gases here instead of allowing them to escape totally into space? Gravity. The ability of a planet to hold its gases depends on its gravitational forces. For a molecule to escape the earth's gravity, it must have an outward velocity of 25,000 miles (40,232 kilometers) per hour and make it through the region of escape. Generally, heavy molecules get that speed by chance. Light molecules, such as helium, can escape the earth's atmosphere. Helium escapes at a mean rate of 1 million years from the time it escapes the earth's crust until it leaves the atmosphere and goes to outer space. Scientists use molecular theory to calculate the escape times of other types of gases that are released as a part of the biogeochemical and geochemical processes on Earth. The components of the atmosphere are as follows:

Troposphere: The part of the atmosphere closest to the earth, ranging from 6.2 to 12.4 miles (10 to 20 kilometers) in height. The troposphere runs from the earth's surface to the tropopause (the boundary between the troposphere and the stratosphere, which varies in height: 9.3 to 12.4 miles (15 to 20 km) in the tropics, to 6.2 miles (10 km) in polar regions. The vertical movement through the troposphere causes climate changes on Earth. The troposphere cools rapidly toward its upper limits, and creates the first of two water traps of the atmosphere because as water rises and cools, it expands and falls back down to Earth (as rain, sleet, or snow).

Ozone Layer (Ozonosphere): The general stratum of the upper atmosphere in which there is an ozone concentration. Here is where the ozone plays an important part in the radiative balance of the atmosphere. The ozone layer lies roughly between 6.2 to 31.5 miles (10 to 50 km) above the surface of the earth, with the maximum ozone concentration at about 12.4 to 15.5 miles (20 to 25 km).

Stratosphere: The atmospheric shell above the troposphere (beginning at the tropopause) and below the mesosphere. Stratospheric radiation occurs in the stratosphere, whereby infrared radiation involved in the complex radiation exchange continually proceeds (in from the sun and back out from the earth). The stratosphere is the second part of the atmosphere that traps water, preventing its loss outward. When a volcano erupts, its particles (mostly sulfur compounds) become trapped in the stratosphere and come down slowly. This generally lowers the earth's temperature by 1.5 degrees C (by reflecting incoming solar radiation).

Exosphere: The outermost region of the atmosphere, estimated at 310 to 621 miles (500 to 1,000 km) where the density is very low. The mean free path of particles depends upon their direction and where the particles are with respect to local vertical in the exosphere (the greatest being for upward traveling particles). Another name for the exosphere is the "region of escape."

Magnetosphere: In the atmosphere the earth's geomagnetic field extends out to about 62 miles (100 km) and then outward to a far boundary where interplanetary space begins. This region of the atmosphere plays an important role in controlling the physical processes that take place in the biosphere. Many scientists agree that the magnetosphere is important for life to exist.

Ionosphere: The part of Earth's upper atmosphere that contains charged particles. Its particles are sufficiently ionized by solar ultraviolet radiation so that the concentration of free electrons affects the propagation of radio waves. The base of the ionosphere is at about 43.5 to 50 miles (70 or 80 km) and it extends to an indefinite height.

Thermosphere: The atmospheric shell that extends from the top of the mesosphere to outer space. It is a region with more or less steadily increasing temperature with height, starting at 43.5 to 50 miles (70 or 80 km). When the solar wind increases, the upper regions of the thermosphere can heat up to thousands of degrees. The thermosphere contains the exosphere and most of the ionosphere.

Mesosphere: The layer of the atmosphere between about 28 to 34 miles (45 to 55 km) and 50 to 59 miles (80 to 95 km). The mesosphere extends from the top of the stratosphere to the mesopause (which starts at the top of the mesosphere and corresponds to the level of minimum temperature at 50 to 59 miles (80 to 95 km). The temperature in the mesosphere generally decreases with altitude (the opposite of what happens in the thermosphere, located closer to the sun). The mesosphere acts as a second water trap.

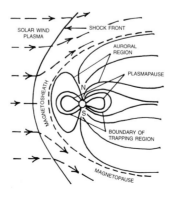

The magnetosphere is shaped like a teardrop, with the bow aimed at the sun. The magnetosphere shields the earth from the sun's powerful solar wind and some cosmic rays that are intercepted by all layers of the atmosphere.

97

During the day when the sun is overhead, the atmosphere scatters mostly blue light waves which is why the sky looks blue. Other colors of light, such as red and violet, are scattered much less than the blue light waves. They come to Earth directly.

Water vapor condenses on particles in the atmosphere creating clouds. Water is trapped in the lower layers of the atmosphere. Otherwise, water would be lost.

At dawn or dusk, when the sun rises and sets, the sky can appear red as the sun reaches a position just below the horizon. When the sun is below the horizon, the light travels through much more of the atmosphere, scattering the blue light waves in such a way that the atmosphere actually absorbs them. Why does the sky look red? Because only the red light reaches us on the surface. The less energetic red rays are bent more than the blue (by the atmosphere which acts like a prism splitting the lightwaves).

98

OBJECTIVE:

Students gain an understanding of the uniqueness of Earth's atmospheric composition.

PROCEDURE:

1. Lead a discussion of the many layers of Earth's atmosphere that are unique to the planet in terms of supporting life in the biosphere (see reference material on pages 96-98).

2. Discuss the differences between the atmospheres of Venus, Earth, and Mars. Note how different the atmosphere of Earth might be if life was not on the planet. (It could be more like Mars.) Ask students to comment on what they think about the way life may affect Earth's atmospheric composition. Refer to the charts below:

NOTE: Other trace gases in the atmosphere include the noble gases helium, argon, krypton, neon, radon, and xenon (listed in order of lightest to heaviest) as well as carbon monoxide, water, methane, and oxides of sulfur and nitrogen.

Composition of Atmosphere	Mars	Venus	Earth Without Life	Earth As Is
Carbon Dioxide	95%	98%	98%	0.034%
Nitrogen	2.7%	1.9%	1.9%	78.08%
Oxygen	0.13%	Trace	Trace	20.95%

Avg. Temperature	Mars	Venus	Earth
Degrees.	-64F/-53C	890F/477C	55F/13C

Distance from the Sun	Mars	Venus	Earth
10^{13} cm	2.29	1.08	1.50

Data from Broecker 1985 and Odum 1989.

3. Ask students to discuss the difference between the carbon dioxide levels in the atmospheres of Earth and Venus. (Encourage students to see the high percentage of nitrogen and oxygen in Earth's atmosphere compared to Venus and Mars. Also, note the low levels of carbon dioxide compared to Venus and Mars.)

4. Ask students how high levels of carbon dioxide and distance from the sun may affect the temperature on the planet. How does temperature correspond to the presence of life? (Mars is too cold for liquids, while Venus is too hot for solids. Life is in a solid form on Earth, and depends on water. Encourage students to see that high temperature range, proximity to the energy source, and atmospheric carbon dioxide levels are interrelated.)

5. Ask students to discuss how the level of atmospheric carbon (in the form of carbon dioxide) stays so low on a planet where living things constantly produce and consume carbon dioxide. Encourage students to discuss the biogeochemical processes, the carbon cycle, and their relationship to the atmosphere.

The rain forest has a 90-foot high ceiling. The mountain inside is 50 feet high.

OBJECTIVE:

Students compare the differences between Biosphere 2's and Earth's atmospheric composition, and how they affect living systems.

PROCEDURE:

1. Invite students to compare the statistics of Biosphere 1 and Biosphere 2. Ask students to describe what they think is the difference between the ratio of air to material (living and nonliving things) in Biosphere 2 compared to what it might be on Earth. Use the following information:

	Biosphere 1	**Biosphere 2**
Land Area	29.2% total area	95% total area
Crust Depth maximum:	44 miles (70 km)	25 feet (7.62 meters)(ocean depth), 17 feet (5.18 meters)(rain forest soil depth)
minimum:	4 miles (6 km)	3.5 feet (1.1 meters)(agricultural area soil depth)
Ocean Area	70.8%	5%
Avg. Ocean Depth	2.2 miles (3.5 km)	20 feet (6 meters)
Atmosphere	400 miles (640 km) high	100 feet (30.5 meters) high

2. Biosphere 2 has approximately 6.534 million cubic feet (185 cubic meters) of air inside all of the biomes, the agricultural area, the micro city, and the technosphere.

3. Challenge students to calculate the area of the earth's atmosphere. The earth's polar diameter is approximately 7,900 miles (12,713 km). Use the calculation $\pi \times r2$ for the area ($\pi = 3.1416$).

For Example:

 Atmosphere + Earth
             - Earth
 _____
      Atmosphere

Atmosphere + Earth (4,350 = radius) 18,922,500 x 3.1416 = 59,446,926 cu. miles
Earth (radius = 3,950)   15,602,500 x 3.1416 = 49,016,814 cu. miles
Atmosphere   10,430,112 cu. miles
Convert the miles into feet (5,280 feet per mile x 10,430,112 miles = 55,070,991,360 cu. feet).

100

4. Invite students to discuss the ways Biosphere 2's atmosphere may be different from Earth's. Discuss ways changes in (1) plant and animal respiration, (2) the water cycle, (3) soil composition, (4) sunlight, and (5) airborne chemicals might affect the balance of gases inside. Students should discuss:

Sunlight on Biosphere 2 is lower in the winter than it is in the summer. This affects carbon dioxide and oxygen levels inside.

• Carbon dioxide production by animals and plants can increase the carbon dioxide levels so they are greater than those in Earth's atmosphere.

• Animals and plants consume oxygen and may need more than what is available in Biosphere 2's atmosphere.

• Low levels of sunlight may cause less oxygen production by the plants, higher levels of carbon dioxide, and lower ocean water pH levels.

• High levels of sunlight can increase oxygen, lower carbon dioxide, and increase the ocean water pH.

• On a hot day, water evaporation can increase, thus increasing the humidity in Biosphere 2.

• Soil disturbances can cause higher carbon dioxide levels in Biosphere 2 if the soil contains a large percentage of composted materials and microorganisms.

• Airborne chemicals, such as paint fumes or gas line fumes, can cause a problem with the balance of gases inside Biosphere 2.

101

The active Augustine volcano.

OBJECTIVE: Students gain an understanding that technology can be used to detect the presence of trace gases that can be missed by human senses (sight and smell), such as radon and carbon monoxide.

MATERIALS NEEDED:

Radon test kit • carbon monoxide test kit (generally available in hardware stores)

PROCEDURE:

1. Lead a discussion of some of the ways the atmosphere changes due to the outgasing of the planet, including:

The geological and chemical processes on the living planet Earth result in the release of gases into the atmosphere. The geochemical activities inside Earth's many layers—from the hot molten core to the outer crust—are on-going, and cause many changes on the surface. The outgasing of the planet causes changes in the atmosphere.

In the biosphere are many forms of matter. Both elements and compounds are in the atmosphere. An element is a substance that does not separate into two (or more) substances by chemical means. A compound can. Elements in their gaseous state in the atmosphere are called noble gases. A form of noble gas is radon. A form of compound is carbon monoxide. Both are in the atmosphere. If either reach high levels in the air of a house, they can pose serious health threats.

2. Show students the radon kit. Explain to students that radon gas, emitted from the earth, gets trapped in houses with underground sections. A radon kit is an inexpensive way to test for radon in the home. Radon is a dangerous noble gas because it is radioactive—that is, it is unstable and splits inside the lungs, causing damage.

3. Demonstrate the radon test kit, following the instructions on the label. Explain that radon is colorless and odorless.

DID YOU KNOW?

Radon is produced from the fission of radium in the earth's crust. The fission produces heat that flows to the earth's surface. The fissioning of radioactive materials in the Earth's crust is similar to a fission power reactor. Both produce heat.

4. Explain to students that another trace gas in the atmosphere is carbon monoxide. This trace gas is a molecule made up of one carbon and one oxygen atom. Carbon monoxide comes from the incomplete burning of materials. A source of carbon monoxide is the burning of petrochemical fuels, such as the carbon monoxide emitted from car exhaust as fuel is being burned in the engine. Carbon monoxide can be deadly.

Carbon monoxide ties up the iron in the blood's hemoglobin so it cannot carry oxygen to the tissues. When bound to the carbon monoxide, the hemoglobin turns a brighter red. Carbon monoxide poisoning will turn a person's lips cherry red. Carbon monoxide has 200 times the affinity for hemoglobin than oxygen. It is difficult for the body to reverse the process. Tests are available to check for carbon monoxide in the home. Ask students: *How would you think carbon monoxide could get into a house?* (Exhaust from a car in the garage, exhaust from a furnace, improperly vented fireplace, cigarette smoke, etc.)

Many homes are tested for carbon monoxide and radon with simple tests.

5. Show students the carbon monoxide test kit. Explain that carbon monoxide is colorless and odorless. Tests vary. You can get inexpensive, disposable kits or sophisticated, high-tech monitors, depending on the purpose of the test. Demonstrate the carbon monoxide test, following the instruction on the label.

6. Explain to students that trace gases are monitored in Biosphere 2 to ensure they do not reach dangerous levels. Unlike inside a house, where the windows can be opened to air the house out, Biosphere 2 is tightly sealed. It does not get aired out due to the sensitivity of many of the experiments scientists conduct inside. Biosphere 2 has a machine called a "sniffer" which detects biogenic gases, such as carbon monoxide and methane. Through the use of many technologies, the scientists monitor the air quality in Biosphere 2 to keep track of the air mixture before any of the gases get out of balance.

103

OBJECTIVE:

Students ask and answer questions related to the ways living systems interact with the atmosphere.

OVERVIEW: The activities on the following pages provide students with ways to discover how aquatic and terrestrial species interact with the atmosphere. The underwater experiment is designed to show students that plants, such as pondweed, consume carbon dioxide from the water and produce gases that go back into the atmosphere. The terrestrial experiment is another visual discovery activity. Students can see that in the process of respiration and transpiration, water vapor escapes into the atmosphere.

MATERIALS NEEDED/EACH TEAM:

Large bowl (4 qt. min.) • glass jar • 4 strands of pondweed (available in some pet stores) • water • magnifying glass

PROCEDURE:

1. Lead a discussion with the students on the ways living things, such as plants, interact with the atmosphere. Include the following:

The biosphere is the thin layer around the planet that includes life and its life support systems. Within this layer, the living and nonliving systems, the biological, and the geological, interact and exchange energy and matter to nurture and sustain life on Earth. The envelope of the biosphere has physical limits and only goes so far down into the ground and up into the atmosphere. In this small band around Earth, all biogeochemical processes occur.

If you look outside, the plants are living organisms that depend on the soil and atmosphere to sustain life.

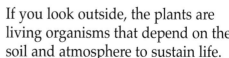

Biosphere 2 aquatic plants take in carbon dioxide and release oxygen.

They also depend on the sun for energy. Plants need air, water, sunlight, and minerals to live and grow in the earth's biosphere. Each part of the plant works to keep the plant alive and growing. Most vascular plants have roots, a stem (or trunk), leaves, and a flower.

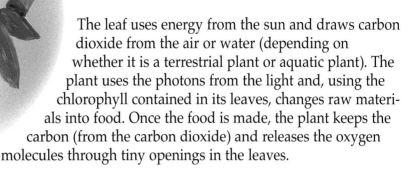

The leaf uses energy from the sun and draws carbon dioxide from the air or water (depending on whether it is a terrestrial plant or aquatic plant). The plant uses the photons from the light and, using the chlorophyll contained in its leaves, changes raw materials into food. Once the food is made, the plant keeps the carbon (from the carbon dioxide) and releases the oxygen molecules through tiny openings in the leaves.

2. Assemble students in small teams. Distribute the materials to the students.

3. Instruct students to fill a bowl with water, then put the jar with pondweed into the bowl. Tilt the jar slightly to fill it with water, then stand the jar upside down. Make sure the pondweed is thoroughly inside the jar.

4. Place the bowl in bright sunlight for a day. Invite students to look for signs of air bubbles on the plant, and document their findings.

5. The next day invite students to view the pondweed for air bubbles again. A magnifying glass is a helpful tool for viewing the bubbles closely. Ask students to document their findings, and compare the amount of air bubbles located on the pondweed to the amount they found on the pondweed the day before.

6. Invite students to share their findings with the class. Ask students to describe what they think caused the bubbles to accumulate near the plant (oxygen given off during the photosynthetic process). Ask students what they think will happen to the bubbles (they will float to the water surface and go up into the atmosphere). Ask students to identify how this activity has shown them how living things interact with the biosphere.

NOTE: Water (H_2O) is consumed in the process of photosynthesis. It is the hydrogen donor to this process which ultimately releases the oxygen through the leaves. The bubbles form on the pondweed in the water. Why? Because oxygen dissolves weakly in water. More oxygen (gas) is produced than can dissolve in the water. Therefore, bubbles form.

105

ACTIVITY

OBJECTIVE: Students ask and answer questions related to the ways living systems interact with the atmosphere.

MATERIALS NEEDED/EACH TEAM:

Leafy plant • water • 2 plastic bags • tape • petroleum jelly • magnifying glass

PROCEDURE:

1. Assemble students in small teams. Distribute the materials to the students.

2. Instruct the students to apply a thin layer of petroleum jelly to the underside of one leaf on the plant. Place a small plastic bag over the leaf, and tape the end of the bag to seal it around the leaf. Leave enough air for the leaf to breathe. Place a small plastic bag over another leaf of similar size on the same plant, and tape the end closely around the leaf.

3. Instruct students to document the condition of the plant, and the conditions inside the bags (dry). Place the plants in a warm, sunny location for one day.

4. Invite students to inspect the plants, and compare the conditions inside each bag. Ask students to document their findings.

5. Invite students to inspect the leaves and bags on the plants. Ask students to document their findings and compare the amount of air bubbles located on the pondweed to the amount they found on the pondweed the day before.

6. Invite students to share their findings with the class. Ask students to describe what they think caused the water vapor to accumulate on the inside of the bag (the oxygen given off during the photosynthetic process also allowed water vapor to escape). Ask students what they think would happen to the water vapor if the bag were not there (the water vapor would go up into the atmosphere). Ask students to identify how this activity has shown them how living things interact with the biosphere.

7. Explain to students that the water vapor escaped through tiny holes in the bottom of the leaves. The opening is a stoma. The stomata allow air exchange (carbon dioxide and oxygen). They also cause a small problem: small molecules of water also escape. The heat of the sun causes water to evaporate and escape through the tiny opening. The stoma is located on the underside of many plants' leaves to keep the openings out of the direct sun (in shade), thus decreasing the evaporation process. The leaves with the petroleum jelly could not breathe. The stomata were coated and sealed. The other leaves were breathing (respiring) and emitting water vapor (transpiring).

8. Invite students to find the stomata, using the magnifying glass.

9. Optional activity: Invite students to research and write a paper on the way(s) water vapor escapes from the bodies of various animals from different ecoregions (Sonoran Desert, Puerto Rican Rain Forest, Sierra Plains, and Rocky Mountains, for example).

Water vapor is often so dense in Biosphere 2 that the water condensate on the windows makes seeing inside to the rain forest very difficult. Evaporation from the ocean equals 700 gallons (2,660 liters) per day.

107

ACTIVITY

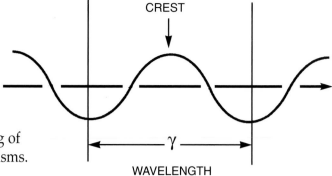

OBJECTIVE: Students gain an understanding of how the sun's light waves affect living organisms.

MATERIALS NEEDED:

Samples of sun screen products

PROCEDURE:

1. One of the most important functions of the earth's atmosphere is that it shields living things from ultraviolet rays from the sun (as well as keeping the temperature from becoming too hot or too cold to support life). Explain to students:

The Earth's sun produces radiation. To us, it is light. Light can be thought of as an oscillating electromagnetic wave, something like a wave moving across a lake. However, a light wave travels at a velocity of 186,420 miles (300,000 kilometers) per second. That's eight times around the earth in one second. There are a variety of light waves. Light waves are characterized by wavelength (the height of the crest of the waves) and frequency (number of waves that pass a point in a second).

Isaac Newton (1642-1727) discovered that sunlight could be broken into its spectral colors of photons of different wavelengths and energies. By the mid 1800s, scientists conducted laboratory experiments and discovered that certain atoms are connected to certain wavelengths, meaning when certain atoms like hydrogen are heated they emit certain photons more than others. They have an emission spectrum. We connect the wavelengths to colors. The longer waves are red. As the waves get shorter, they go through orange, yellow, green, blue, and indigo, then violet. Longer than red are the infrared and radio waves. Shorter than violet are the ultraviolet and gamma rays.

The sun's energy sometimes behaves as a particle. The particle is a photon. Photons supply living things in the biosphere with energy. Light is the main way energy is transported from the sun into the biosphere. The earth's atmosphere protects the living things in the biosphere from damage from the extremely powerful waves, such as the gamma and ultraviolet rays, through its filtering abilities. For example, radio waves will not affect you in the same way as the gamma waves of an atomic bomb. (Gamma ray photons have 10^{15} as much energy as the radio photons.)

The ozone layer offers a great deal of protection from ultraviolet light. Health concerns over the depletion of the ozone layer include that of skin cancer. Ultraviolet light from the sun is linked to skin cancer. The Environmental Protection Agency (EPA) once projected the number of cases of skin cancer through the next 50 years to be 500,000. Of that number, about 9,300 fatalities were expected. That number, updated by the EPA, is estimated at 12 million people who will probably develop skin cancer, and up to 200,000 of them could die. This is an environmental health issue.

Bees need
ultraviolet light
to navigate.

2. Challenge students to calculate how many times greater the new skin cancer rates are than the older ones.

3. Ask students to comment on the environmental link to the health problem.

4. Invite students to describe ways to protect themselves from the risks of skin cancer from ultraviolet light exposure.

5. Demonstrate how to read sun block product labels. Use the samples you are able to acquire.

6. Lead a discussion of ultraviolet light and Biosphere 2, including:

Ultraviolet light does not penetrate the glass panels of Biosphere 2. The difference this may have on the living things inside Biosphere 2 is not completely understood. Without ultraviolet light, the crew members do not get suntans. Humans do not produce vitamin D on their own (people need sunlight to produce healthy levels of vitamin D). The crews that inhabit Biosphere 2 for long periods of time take vitamin D supplements.

Dining in
Biosphere 2.

Insects like bees need ultraviolet light to navigate. Flying to food sources and returning to the hive was too difficult for many of the bees introduced into Biosphere 2. Because the bees failed to pollinate the plants in the biomes and the agricultural area, the crew had to hand-pollinate some crops (like squash) and plants.

Ultraviolet light is needed by some living things, as shown by these two examples. The extent of the needs is yet to be defined. Biosphere 2 is expected to provide scientists with the long-term study opportunities for discovering more about how the earth—and everything in its biosphere—works.

109

Earth as viewed from the moon.

OBJECTIVE: Students gain an awareness of the structure and function of Earth's atmosphere by comparing atmospheric systems of other planets that do not possess biospheres.

MATERIALS NEEDED/EACH TEAM:

Copy of Planetary Analysis worksheet (see page 111)

PROCEDURE:

1. Assemble students in five teams to work on planetary studies together. Copy and distribute the student worksheets to the teams. Assign each team one planet.

2. Lead a discussion of the uniqueness of Earth's atmosphere for keeping the planet's biological systems alive, including:

Earth is one of the few planets whose atmosphere has elements in liquid, gas, and solid form (otherwise known as the triple point). On Earth, water appears in liquid, gas (vapor), and solid (ice) forms. Earth's atmosphere works like a greenhouse. Temperature and humidity produce a comfortable environment, hospitable for living things. The greenhouse effect is the capture of infrared light reflected off sizable portions of Earth (e.g., oceans). Water vapor, methane, carbon dioxide, and nitrous oxide in the atmosphere capture the reflected light and warm the earth. The temperature of a planet depends on the sunlight, plus the reflective properties on the surface and the infrared light-absorbing gases in its atmosphere. Water vapor is the most important absorber of reflected infrared light in the atmosphere. Clouds contain water vapor and droplets. They play an important role in reflecting the sunlight.

3. Invite students to compare the atmosphere of Earth to that of the planet assigned to their team. Challenge students to answer these questions through research and cooperative discussions: *Can life survive on this planet? What is your reason(s) for this answer?* Encourage students to look for facts and to construct a presentation of their information that supports their argument, using scientific publications, interviews, and previous learning.

Assessment Suggestion

Students should be able to articulate positions on the reasons the planets are inhabitable, including: large amounts of greenhouse gases in the atmospheres, lack of water, and extreme temperature ranges.

1. My Team is assigned this planet: _____

2. Keep facts about the planet here:

Look for the planet's general characteristics, such as atmosphere, presence of water, soil characteristics, temperatures, and light levels.

3. Can life survive on this planet?

4. What are your reasons for this answer?

TIPS

Mercury has no atmosphere.

Venus has a thick yellowish cloud cover over the whole planet. Its atmosphere is primarily carbon dioxide. Water vapor is barely detectable.

Mars is a small dry planet, with a primarily carbon dioxide atmosphere.

Jupiter has thick clouds of hydrogen made of liquids and gases.

Neptune, with an atmosphere that is mainly methane gas, has a blue atmosphere with three rings.

111

BIOSPHERE 2 SOIL FACTS

• The soils inside Biosphere 2 were collected in Arizona.

• The soils were blended by soil scientists into different soil types for the rain forest, desert, savannah, marine areas, and agricultural area.

Studies were made and special soils were mixed for the plant communities. Soil containing highly organic material (from a cattle watering hole) was used in the agricultural area.

112

Sand was brought into the United States from the Bahamas. It is a white carbonate sand used in the ocean.

**TOTAL WEIGHT OF
BIOSPHERE 2 SOILS:**

30,000 TONS

(27.2 million KG)

**TOTAL NUMBER OF
DIFFERENT TYPES OF
SOIL:**

18

Soils were carefully placed in
Biosphere 2's rain forest.

113

Erosion in Bryce Canyon.

OBJECTIVE:

Students gain a basic understanding of the importance of soils in the biogeochemical cycles in the biosphere.

MATERIALS NEEDED/EACH TEAM:

Jar with lid (1) • water • dry sand • backyard soil • potting soil

PROCEDURE:

1. Lead a discussion on soils in the biosphere, including:

Soil is one of the greatest resources on Earth. The soil consists of chemically altered rock fragments (usually very small) that are mixed with organic materials, such as plant growth and animal matter. Soil is the stratum below the vegetation and above the hard rock in the biosphere, including loose material from weathered rock (devoid of plants) to thick humus and soil mixtures (rich in organic matter). The pH of soils ranges from alkaline to acidic, depending on the chemical elements in the organic and mineral matter.

The important function of this layer of the earth's land surface is that the soil holds water and nutrient supply for plants. Plants are critical for higher members of the food chain and food webs of an ecosystem. If it were not for the soil, most plants would not be able to secure their roots, acquire water and nutrients, and take in air. The granites of the continents contain aluminum, sodium, and potassium—all of which play a minor role in the earth's mantle. The ocean floor is different: It is more like the mantle, and is more abundant in iron and magnesium.

A soil scientist checks the rain forest soil.

The age of these substances are different, too. Scientists believe the oceans' basalts are 0.1 billion years in age, while the continental granites were probably formed around 3.8 billion years ago.

The earth is considered geologically alive. Molten material flows from the center of the planet upward. Volcanoes erupt, and molten rock pours forth to Earth's crust. Most volcanoes are located along the tectonic plates. Solid material is returned to the center at subduction zones (a place where one crustal block descends beneath another, such as the Pacific plate descends under the Andean plate).

The flux of heat between the earth's internal core and the surface varies greatly. For example, six feet down in the temperate zone, the temperature is about 54 degrees F (12 degrees C) depending on the time of the year (winter or summer). Yet one mile down, the temperature is 120 degrees F (49 degrees C), and it increases with depth. This is not heat from the sun. It is caused by internal fissioning.

2. Invite students to discuss the similarities and differences between life above ground and in the soil. For example, life above and below ground require oxygen, food, water, and living space. Movement in the soil is less than it can be above ground, due to penetration ability. The temperature in the ground is more constant than it is above ground. Soil protects the organisms from wind, light levels, and evaporation. Water (from heavy rains) can soak and fill the air spaces in the soil, forming a zone where no oxygen is available for its inhabitants.

3. Optional Demonstration: Bring in samples of local soils, and invite students to compare textures, identify organic matter, and look at colors, granule sizes, etc.

4. Optional Activity: Invite students to monitor the temperature in the ground and in the air. They should do this at home on a weekend, checking the temperature in the morning, afternoon, and evening for a day.

5. Optional Activity: Have teams of students mix 1/4 cup sand, 1/4 cup potting soil, and 1/4 cup backyard soil in the jar. Fill the jar 2/3 full with water. Seal the jar, and shake well. Set the jars down, and let the soil settle. The heaviest particles will settle to the bottom. The sand layer will form first. It can take up to 24 hours for the sand and silt particles to settle. Ask students to describe why it is important for the sand to settle on the bottom.

115

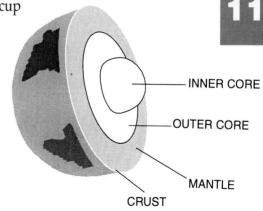

INNER CORE

OUTER CORE

MANTLE

CRUST

OBJECTIVE:

Students gain a greater understanding of the diversity of soils in the biosphere.

MATERIALS NEEDED/EACH TEAM:

Dry sand • backyard soil • potting soil • stopwatch • 3 glass jars • cups (plastic or paper) • 3 cups water • measuring cup • pencil and paper

PROCEDURE:

1. Explain that this activity will allow the students to see how different soils drain differently. Distribute the materials. Invite students to inspect the three soil types, and write predictions about which soil will drain the fastest and the slowest.

2. Tell students to punch small holes into the bottom of each cup. Set the cup in the top of the jar, and tape the cup to the jar. Place three small, equally sized punctures in the bottoms of the cups (for drainage).

3. Fill a cup 1/2 full of sand. Pour 1 cup of water into the cup. Using a stopwatch, measure the amount of time it takes for the water to drain through the sand and into to the jar. Write "Sand" and the time on a sheet of paper.

4. Fill a cup 1/2 full of potting soil. Pour 1 cup of water into the cup. Using a stopwatch, measure the amount of time it takes for the water to drain through the sand and into to jar. Write "Potting Soil" and the time on a sheet of paper.

5. Fill a cup 1/2 full of backyard soil. Pour 1 cup of water into the cup. Using a stopwatch, measure the amount of time it takes for the water to drain through the sand and into to jar. Write "Backyard Soil" and the time on a sheet of paper.

6. Invite student teams to share their findings. Write the time on a board for the class to see and compare. Ask students to discuss the reasons why one type of soil might drain faster (on the average) (e.g., size of soil particles and spaces between can speed and slow water movement; organic materials can absorb water).

7. Tell students to measure the amount of water in each jar, and write their findings for sand, potting soil, and backyard soil. Keep the soils, cups, and jars for the experiment on page 120.

Moving soils into position in Biosphere 2 required the use of heavy equipment.

8. Invite student teams to share their findings. Ask students to discuss the reasons why there are variations in the amount of water that drained through the cup (same as above).

9. Explain to students that there are two soil groups in Biosphere 2: a topsoil and a subsoil. The topsoil is three to five feet thick, and varies from biome to biome. For example, the topsoil in the savannah and rain forest are rich in clay and retain water. The topsoil in the desert is very sandy and rocky. The subsoil in Biosphere 2 is nearly 15 feet thick. It allows water to drain. The term used to describe the gravity flow of ground water through the pore spaces in soil is called "percolation." The movement of water through the soil systems is a significant (and on-going) biogeochemical process that occurs in the biosphere.

10. Invite students to discuss how pollution (living microorganisms, pesticides, and herbicides, for example) could enter ground water supplies by traveling through the soil. Encourage students to research contemporary examples of this problem and share their findings with the class.

11. Optional Activity: Invite students to write a paper on a flood and what caused the flood to occur.

Suggested Assessment

Students should be able to convey their awareness of soil having variation and being integral to the biogeochemical processes in the biosphere.

117

ACTIVITY

OBJECTIVE:

Students gain an awareness of the relationship between soil particle shapes, air, and plant root systems.

MATERIALS NEEDED/EACH TEAM:

Magnifying glass • potting soil • backyard soil • sand • variety of house and vegetable plants • notebook and pencils

PROCEDURE:

1. Lead a discussion on the relationship between soil composition, air availability, and plant growth, including:

It is important for plants to have air in the soil, especially oxygen. Roots breathe in oxygen and breathe out carbon dioxide. There are many types of soils, from loose sand to heavy clay. In heavy soil, the spaces between the particles are very tight. These are called the "pore spaces." Sand has large pore spaces. Clay has small pore spaces.

In Biosphere 2 it is important for scientists to know what kind of soil they are working with in each biome. You might say the soil needs to have good drainage, but what is good drainage? How does water move through the soil so that the plants' roots can breathe? Scientists also look at the amount of organic matter in the soil. Organic matter and minerals provide plants with essential nutrients that are water soluble (so they can be absorbed by the roots).

Plant roots adapt to the conditions of their environment. For example, the red and black mangrove trees found in the Florida Everglades have part of their root systems above ground in the water. When the tide recedes, the root is exposed to the air. The roots breathe in oxygen during this time, for the soil below the water is saturated.

2. Assemble students into teams. Distribute samples of the sand, potting soil, and backyard soil, as well as the magnifying glass. Encourage students to draw and describe the differences among the three types of soils. Ask students: *What do you see? How are the shapes different? How might the shapes influence the amount of air that can be available for the roots of the plants?*

118

3. Distribute plants to the students. Instruct students to take the plants out of the pots and gently remove the soil from the roots with their hands, being careful not to tear the roots. Invite the students to compare the root systems of all plants. Challenge students to describe (in writing) what they think is the reason for the shape of the root, then go to the library and find the type of soil best suited for the plant species. After the students find out what soil type the plant prefers, invite students to explain why it prefers that soil, based on the root system configuration.

4. Invite the students to explore an outdoor area. Look for evidence of roots needing to breathe. Some will be above ground, some below. Ask students to search for places that do not have plants growing, and to explain why plants do not grow in those soils (the soils are too hard, too wet, too dry; not enough nutrients; pollution; erosion). Encourage students to take a close look, using the magnifying glass, and describe what they see in a field notebook.

Suggested Assessment

Students should be able to identify the relationship between the soil environment and the root system configuration of plants that may be influenced by the plants' need to access air passages, need to access water sources, and ability to move through the soil.

OBJECTIVE:

Students observe the effects of soil variations on plant growth.

MATERIALS NEEDED/EACH TEAM:

Potting soil (sterile)* • backyard soil* • sand* • 3 cups* • 3 jars* • water • paper towel • plastic bags with closures • pea, bean, and alfalfa seeds (8 each) • ruler • measuring cup • pencils • tape • labels • copy of student worksheet (see page 121)

* Recycle the soils used in the experiment on page 116.

PROCEDURE:

1. Distribute the materials to each team of students. Instruct students to moisten the paper towels and place the pea, bean, and alfalfa seeds in the towels. Place the seeds in a warm location, until six of each type of seed sprout. Keep the towels moist.

2. Instruct students to assemble the cups onto the jars, as in the soil drainage experiment on page 116. Moisten the soil in the cups. Dig six small holes, 1/2 inch deep, in each cup. Plant two pea, bean, and alfalfa seedlings in each cup. Gently cover the roots with the soil. Label each soil sample with the type of soil and the team's name for identification. Use the seedlings in the potting soil as the control.

3. Ask students to predict which plants have the greatest chance of survival—the sand or the backyard soil, and state the reason why on their data sheet.

4. Tell students to write the date and measure the height of each plant on the data sheet for the next 14 days. Keep the experiments in a warm, sunny location. Instruct the students to check the soils each day to make sure the plants have adequate moisture. When students add water, ask them to measure and document the amount of water they add in the "Water" category in the correct day/date category of the data sheet.

5. After 14 days, invite the students to prepare a paper describing the results of their experiment. Encourage students to check the roots of each plant and comment on the soil composition, the structure, and the possible reasons why some of the plants did better than others.

Suggested Assessment

Students should be able to identify the effects of soil variations on plant growth.

Team name: _____

Prediction: _____

	SAND				BACKYARD SOIL				POTTING SOIL			
	Peas	Beans	Alfalfa	Water	Peas	Beans	Alfalfa	Water	Peas	Beans	Alfalfa	Water
Day 1 Date:												
Day 2 Date:												
Day 3 Date:												
Day 4 Date:												
Day 5 Date:												
Day 6 Date:												
Day 7 Date:												
Day 8 Date:												
Day 9 Date:												
Day 10 Date:												
Day 11 Date:												
Day 12 Date:												
Day 13 Date:												
Day 14 Date:												

NOTE: When you add water, write the amount you added and the date in the "water" category.

SECTION 4

The Classroom Biosphere

Experiential Elements: This six-part activity contains the essential elements of small-scale biospheric design and study. Students work in teams, as do members of the Biosphere 2 staff, to research, plan, construct, monitor, measure, and analyze data. Students gain an understanding of how their decisions impact the performance of the system they design through discussions, hands-on experience, reading, research, data collection, and data analysis. Science can be fun and challenging. The reason the instructions for building a biosphere are general is to encourage students to be creative within the framework of the experiment.

This module is intended to be administered after the students have participated in the discussions and activities contained in Sections 1 through 3. The individual studies should prepare them for designing and studying ecosystems in the classroom. These studies will help the students understand the purpose of the experiment and relate the small-scale simulation to some of the challenges the Biosphere 2 scientists and technologists face in researching the ways biospheres work.

OVERVIEW: This section provides a framework to enable students to cooperate with others to gain an understanding of systems, diversity, and interactions by collecting, organizing, and analyzing relevant data to make informed decisions. Before the activities begin, it is best to decide how many classroom sessions, or how much time, to allocate to each activity. Best results are achieved if students have a minimum number of supplies provided, which permits groups to accomplish the entire program without having to bring supplies to class. Students can be encouraged to bring materials. It is up to you. Other tips are included on this page.

TEACHER'S CHECK LIST:

Make decisions related to the length of the experiment phases.
Recommended allowance (days = class periods @ 1 hour/period):

> 1 - 3 days for research
> 2 days for planning
> 1 - 2 days for constructing
> 7 days minimum for monitoring
> 1 - 2 days for calculations and conclusions

Identify the materials students will be provided and/or permitted to use in building a classroom biosphere. Students should use materials that do not emit harmful gases. For example, duct tape and glass may be better than glue, adhesives, or sealants. Recommendation: Provide students with basic materials to develop a functional project, and permit optional use of soils, waters, species and structures.

Determine the technologies and methods appropriate for student use during the monitoring phase (scales, rulers, computers, pH tests, microscopes, etc.).

Suggestion: Encourage students to keep log books to document their observations throughout the six phases of the activity. You may want to allow students to try large enclosures, even greenhouses, if available. You may want to encourage students to use invertebrates in their projects. Always consider humane handling and care of living things used in any activity.

MATERIALS NEEDED:

You will need to make a set of copies of these worksheets for each team of students.

Student Worksheet: Research (page 132)

Student Worksheet: Plan (page 133)

Student Worksheet: Construct (page 134)

Student Worksheet: Monitor (page 135)

Student Worksheet: Calculate & Conclude (page 136)

The architects who designed Biosphere 2 spent years researching technical needs of the project.

OBJECTIVE: Students gain experience formulating questions and searching for answers in a cooperative environment.

NOTE: This activity requires at least one to three classroom sessions to provide time for students to research the topics and engage in dialogue.

MATERIALS NEEDED/EACH TEAM:

Copy of all student worksheets (see page 132 - 135)• classroom biosphere container, soil, water, and species for ecosystem design reference

PROCEDURE:

1. Group students into teams of three to five people. Students should work in the same groups throughout the experiment.

2. Distribute and review all the student worksheets (see pages 132 - 135). Explain the project parameters you have established for the experiment, including all deadlines for completing the six phases of the activity.

3. Direct students to (1) follow the instructions on the Research worksheet, (2) make decisions regarding the type of ecosystem that will be in their biosphere, (3) develop a hypothesis, and (4) perform research to decide what could be needed. Explain that the research is a preface to designing a model of the biosphere they construct and to conducting further research.

4. Encourage the students to think in terms of a systems approach, so they will need to know how living things interact with their environment.

5. Ask students to identify any scientific or technological achievements that influenced their team's choices during the research phase.

OBJECTIVE: Extend the team activities so students learn to cooperate with others to use their imagination, creativity, decision-making, and communication skills to set goals and develop plans.

MATERIALS NEEDED/EACH TEAM:

Copy of student worksheet: "Plan" (see page 133)
• classroom biosphere container, soil, water, and species for ecosystem design reference

PROCEDURE:

NOTE: This activity needs a minimum of two classroom sessions.

1. Review the student worksheet: "Plan" with the students.

2. Group students into their teams to develop their plan, using the worksheets as a guide (it is not all-inclusive; invite students to expand on the general guidelines).

3. Encourage students to recall and review the Biosphere 2 studies from Sections 1 through 3. They have studied many important environmental factors and have been given many clues for planning a biosphere.

4. If you are providing the students with materials for the project, make them available as a reference for students. This may help them develop the drawings, plans, and predictions more accurately.

5. Tell students that they will compare their results to their plans later, so it is important for them to be as specific as possible in the planning stage of building their biosphere (i.e., what they plan to study and how they will study it). Students should reference "Monitor"and "Calculate" worksheets for suggestions on what type of data collection they might include in the plan.

6. Ask students to:
• State the goal of their experiment.

• Write out their plan and identify the ecosystem, the species diversity, the structure, and the function of the experiment.

• Identify as many environmental factors as needed for their biosphere to sustain life, including the methods they will use to make sure the environment is appropriate for their ecosystem.

• Define how their experiment relates to local or worldwide environmental research. They may want to model the project after one they found during their research, for example.

• Describe the interactions they think will occur between the soil, plants, animals, water, air, and other elements of their biosphere, such as recycling.

ACTIVITY

*B*iosphere 2 "openings" and "closures" attract many members of the media.

OBJECTIVE:

Students use an organized approach, learn to apply experimental design concepts, and gain hands-on experience building a classroom biosphere while cooperating with others.

MATERIALS NEEDED/EACH TEAM:

Copy of student worksheet: "Construct" (see page 134) • classroom biosphere container with a clear, thick plastic cover, tape, soil, water, and species for ecosystem construction

PROCEDURE:

NOTE: This activity could take one to two classroom sessions.

1. Review the student worksheet: "Construct" (page 134) with the students.

2. Group students into the same teams of three to five to construct their biospheres, according to their plans.

NOTE: Part of the construction process can include the physical collection of materials, soil, water, and species from a nearby ecosystem. Provide time in the construction phase for collection as well as construction if all resources are not made available in the classroom.

3. Before the biosphere is sealed (if this is a sealed experiment), students should take baseline readings of the environmental factors they plan to monitor (e.g., temperature, pH levels) and document the condition of the living species they see. If microscopes are available, encourage students to sample part of their experiments and document their findings under the microscope.

4. Tell students to compare their construction to the plan and document the challenges they faced during the construction phase. Ask students to describe differences between the plan and the actual construction. Suggest that students review their hypotheses and evaluation methods. Will they work with this biosphere?

OPTIONAL WRITING ACTIVITY:

You can challenge the students to write a press release that will announce the closure of their biosphere, using newspaper-style writing. Tell them to answer the readers' questions including "Who?" (the team), "What?" (the experiment), "When?" (the date of closure and the date of opening), "Where?" and "Why?" in the opening paragraph of the press release.

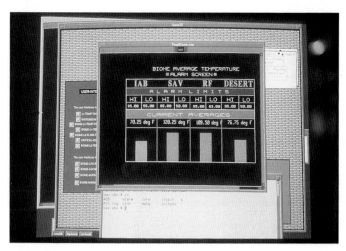

Computers monitor temperature changes in Biosphere 2.

OBJECTIVE: Students cooperate with others to gain experience collecting, organizing, and analyzing data; formulating questions about nature to solve problems; and explaining phenomena using scientific concepts.

MATERIALS NEEDED/EACH TEAM:

1 per student: copy of student worksheet: "Monitor" (see page 135)
• biosphere projects

PROCEDURE:

NOTE: This activity should be allowed to be conducted for at least five to ten classroom sessions—long enough for visible results and problem solving opportunities to arise.

1. Review the "Monitor" worksheets (see page 135) with the students.

2. Tell students to work in their teams to collect data on their biosphere following their plans.

3. If the students have not taken a baseline reading (i.e., this is not a sealed experiment), direct them to take baseline readings of the environmental factors they plan to monitor (e.g., temperature, pH levels) and document the conditions of the living species they see. If microscopes are available, encourage the students to study elements of their experiment under the microscope and document their findings.

4. While the students are performing the monitoring tasks, check on each team's biosphere and encourage the students to discuss their daily findings (informally). Use this opportunity to encourage discussion of changes or observable processes that you see the group may have missed.

5. As part of the monitoring process, encourage the students to evaluate the impact of their experiment's design. Invite them to inquire: "Is it working? Is it not working?" Because ecosystems are complex, students can gain a better understanding of how they work if faced with solving problems rather than simply monitoring this experiment.

A Biospherian uses the computer in Biosphere 2.

6. If an ecosystem appears to be in danger, you may want to provide the student team with an opportunity to explore and modify the experiment. To study cause-and-effect relationships, encourage students, as follows:

• Identify the problem (effect).

• Identify the cause of the problem.

• Assess the impact (or extent of the damage).

• Identify a possible solution, based on formal or informal research.

• Define the specific approach for modifying the experiment, including a prediction of the effects of the change.

• Perform the modification according to the plan.

• Monitor the change.

NOTE: Return the life forms to their natural environment if the experiment fails.

7. Optional: If computers are available, encourage students to use them for word processing or spreadsheet documentation. Biosphere 2 scientists use computers. Inside Biosphere 2 it is a "paperless society" because the paper cannot be recycled.

Scientists continue research calculations and conclusions in Biosphere 2. It is a long-term project, designed to last 100 years.

OBJECTIVE: Students cooperate with others to express results and explain phenomena by relying on data, facts, observations, and scientific concepts.

MATERIALS NEEDED:

Copy of student worksheet: "Calculate & Conclude" (see page 136)
• biosphere project

PROCEDURE:

NOTE: This activity may take one to two classroom sessions to permit adequate time for students to prepare their calculations and conclusions.

1. Review the "Calculate & Conclude" worksheet (see page 136) with the students.

2. Direct students to work in their teams to calculate data from the classroom biospheres using their data, facts, and observations combined with scientific concepts.

3. Tell students to develop a conclusion (formal or informal, depending on your requirements). The basic conclusion should (1) explain the results achieved, (2) describe consistencies or deviations from the plan, and (3) provide a conclusive statement of what the team learned from the project.

4. Challenge students to draw a comparison between their biosphere's performance and similar issues facing the environment (local or global) as part of their conclusion.

5. Optional Activity: Invite students to share their scientific environmental research with the community by writing a story for a local paper that may help readers become more aware of the environment and/or how to act more responsibly toward the environment.

BUILD A BIOSPHERE

To build your own biosphere experiment you need to start with soil, air, and water. . . the media that support the "bios" (life) in the biosphere. Decide what is important. For example, the medium has to be habitable for life. In your experiment, there is a food web you'll need to consider. Try to design your experiment so that it sustains life without calling out for pizza. Try to grow the food the inhabitants need inside your biosphere experiment, just as in Biosphere 2.

Select a single ecosystem for your biosphere experiment. An ecosystem is a system that has input and output by the living and nonliving things that are knit together as an organized unit. The input can be the energy from the sun or water in the form of rain into the ecological unit. The output is what the ecological unit produces, such as heat, carbon dioxide, oxygen, or wastes.

In the middle of the input and output, your biosphere is consuming. That's why the ecosystem in your biosphere needs a food web. Members of the food web either produce or consume. If your biosphere project has a large consumer, like a mouse, a turtle, or a fish, you must make sure there are enough plants or animals (or both) to meet that animal's needs by producing enough food so that the consumer can live.

If you throw a bunch of plants, soil, water, and creatures into a glass container and seal it, you can have a pretty wild project. However, it probably will last only a little while. If you want to build a biosphere that will support life, well, that's another story. Research and understanding are key. For the experiment:

• Pick an ecosystem. It can be from your area, or it can be from another place on the planet. Try to find a similar experiment or environmental problem in the news you can model your experiment on. Maybe you can solve the problem.

• Research the needs of the ecosystem. Air, water, and soil are important. So is selection (you can purchase many seeds and plants to go into your biosphere). Research the needs of insects, fungi, and microorganisms. Keep records of your research.

• When you determine the species you want, go to the library and research the type of food and the amount you'll need to sustain life in your classroom biosphere. Figure out which members of the food web should be in the ecosystem to keep everything alive. You may need to have an "import" for food, like worms, for an animal higher on the food chain to eat.

• Research the size of your biosphere. Size is relevant to food production, right? Even a field mouse could be a challenge. You must have 10 to 100 times the biomass of the mouse in grass for one field mouse.

• Research the environmental needs of the biosphere. How much water will it need? What is the pH of the soil? Is temperature a big deal? Lighting?

• State your hypothesis as a preliminary step to the next phase: planning.

The plans for building Biosphere 2 included the collection of plants from around the world. This photo shows some of the desert plants.

Once the research is done, put the facts together and figure out where to get the species for the biosphere project and how they will be contained. Put a plan together that includes the biosphere design, the materials, soil, water, and air, as well as the plants and animals that will live inside. You are building a human-controlled, enclosed ecosystem called a mesocosm. You might:

• Write a goal for your biosphere, such as what you want to achieve with the life-sustaining project. See "Calculate" worksheet for ideas on data collection. Gathering information in the form of measurements provides you with something to use in calculating percentages, charting, or making quantifiable statements. Written descriptions are valuable references for scientists, especially ones like you who want to remember how a species changed (for instance, color, leaf shapes, etc.).

• Write a description of the ecosystem the biosphere is to represent, and state what you are going to do to make sure it represents that ecosystem.

• Define how your experiment relates to local or worldwide environmental research.

• Write or draw a description of the air, waste, and water recycling systems in your biosphere.

• Draw a diagram of the biosphere structure and a map of the soil, plants, body of water, etc.

• Write a plan for constructing the biosphere. Include a list of the items and amounts, the type of soil, temperature ranges, and the species. Include all the other things your classroom biosphere will need.

• Identify as many environmental factors as needed for the biosphere's environment to sustain life.

• Write a prediction for your biosphere. Describe the interactions you think will occur between the soil, plants, animals, water, air, and other elements of the biosphere, such as recycling.

Biosphere 2 "openings" and "closures" attract many members of the media.

Construct the biosphere using a clear container with a "sample" taken from a local ecological unit (as scientists did with the Florida Everglade samples for Biosphere 2 marsh) or your own carefully assembled ecological unit. Try grown seedlings or plants, a healthy water supply, soil with microorganisms and other life—everything you think you'll need based on your research and plan. Here are some hints:

• Glass jars (with lids) can be used for small biospheres. You're recycling at the same time! Make sure the glass is very clean before you build the biosphere. An aquarium tank is another way to contain your biosphere project. To create a closed aquarium, secure a tight-fitting lid (and seal it with tape).

• Collect the species, according to your plan.

• Insects can be captured in nets or containers or by hand. Having a hard time finding them? Try using lights or setting food out to attract them or going to their food sources to find them. Make sure they meet your ecosystem needs.

• Be humane to all living things you use. Do not use endangered or threatened species in your experiment, please.

• Here is a sample food chain:

detritus → pill bug → centipede

A Biospherian
uses the computer
in Biosphere 2.

Monitor means to check. Monitor your experiments and write each observation. This is data collecting, something very important in science. As a part of the scientific research you are performing in this biosphere project, record as much as you can about the state of the biosphere at the beginning of the experiment. Then make periodic checks and tests, depending on the rules you create for the experiment. Make a final check at the end of the experiment to compare aspects of your biosphere "before" and "after."

Monitoring ideas:

• Take temperature readings at the same time each day, or several times a day.

• Check the quality of the soil and water used in your biosphere. Inexpensive and simple kits to test nutrient contents can be bought in hardware and gardening stores. Try the pH test. It's fun!

• Population check: count the plants and animals by species. Record the numbers.

• Measure the heights of the plants, and draw pictures to document physical changes.

WORKSHEET

Scientists continue research calculations and conclusions in Biosphere 2. It is a long-term project, designed to last 100 years.

CALCULATE:

To measure the results of the experiment, take the data (observations, pictures, temperatures, population records, pH or water quality tests, etc.) and see what has changed or stayed the same in the biosphere. The measurements and recordings you make will help define the change. For example:

• You can calculate growth in plants (from measurements).

• You can calculate declining populations (from counting and recording).

• You can calculate increasing populations (from counting and recording).

• You can calculate percentages of surviving species.

• You can graph and compare changes in temperature, lighting, pH, and water quality.

CONCLUDE:

Develop a conclusion. In order to explain the project results, you may want to research possible causes. Talk to experts, go to the library and research, refer to your notes and work from previous (similar) experiments, or share information with other groups. This conclusion can:

• Explain the results using data, facts, and observations.

• Explain the scientific concepts at work in your biosphere.

• Explain similarities and differences between your research and the environmental research scientists are doing locally or worldwide.

• Explain what your team learned from the project.

• Look at the reasons your biosphere plan worked or did not work.

• Were you able to identify any "cause-and-effect" relationships to explain changes that occurred during the experiment?

• Present facts on the changes that occurred or processes you saw (water cycles, decomposition of material, etc.).

GLOSSARY
&
REFERENCES

BIODEGRADABLE: capable of being decomposed by living organisms, especially microbes such as bacteria.

BIOMES: large portions of the earth with similar nonliving (climate, soil) and living (plant and animal communities) components.

BIOSPHERE 1: the thin surface layer of the earth's outer crust, its water, and the air containing all life.

BIOSPHERE 2: a 3.15-acre miniature replica of Earth, including six biomes, designed as a 100-year experiment to understand how Biosphere 1 supports life and recycles all its water, air, waste, nutrients, and minerals.

CARBON DIOXIDE: one of Earth's biogenic gases that is important to plant and animal life.

CONDENSATION: part of the water cycle in which gas or vapor cools and changes to a liquid (denser form) while giving off energy.

CONTROLLED STUDY: a scientific experiment using a control condition and experimental condition(s) in which a variable is manipulated and the results are monitored.

CORAL REEF: a rocklike growth consisting mostly of calcium carbonate skeletons made by animals (coral polyps) in warm sea water.

DECOMPOSER: a bacterium or fungus that causes the rot or decay (chemical breakdown) of organic matter.

DESALINATION: the process of removing salt from sea water.

ECOSYSTEM: a self-supporting community of living organisms and their living and nonliving environment.

ESTUARY: the marshy area and tide where a river or stream joins a large salt-water lake, sea, or ocean.

EVAPORATION: the part of the water cycle in which water changes from a liquid to a gas or vapor at a temperature below the boiling point.

EVAPO-TRANSPIRATION: the process by which water vapor escapes from a living plant, primarily its leaves and stems, and enters the atmosphere.

FOOD CHAIN: a group of living things that form a chain in which the first is eaten by the second, etc.; the sequence of energy transfer in the form of food when one organism from one trophic level eats or decomposes another.

FOOD WEB: an interlocking system of food chains.

GERMINATION: the process that occurs when a plant embryo begins growing or sprouts from a seed, using its stored energy.

LIFE-SUPPORT SYSTEMS: mechanisms, natural or man-made, that enable living things to survive.

LIMITING FACTOR: a component of the environment that limits the size and reproductive success of a population.

MICROBE/MICROORGANISM: a microscopic organism (such as a bacterium) necessary in nutrient recycling, as a producer, consumer, or decomposer.

NUTRIENT: a substance/raw material needed for the growth and development of organisms.

pH: a scale to measure the negative log of the concentration of the hydrogen ions in a substance, expressed as acid, neutral, or base (alkaline).

PHOTOSYNTHESIS: the process by which plants with chlorophyll convert light energy into chemical energy (e.g., use sunlight, water, and carbon dioxide to release oxygen and simple sugar).

PRECIPITATION: the part of the water cycle in which water is deposited on Earth (as rain, hail, mist, sleet, or snow).

RECYCLING: the process by which resources are made fit to be used again.

RESEARCH: rigorous inquiry to search for causes (i.e., controlled experiments), for concomitants (i.e., study relationships for predictive purposes), for description (case study methods of observation), and for simulation modeling (for extrapolation and prediction).

RESPIRATION: the process of breathing by animals whereby oxygen is taken in, stored energy is used for food, and water and carbon dioxide are released.

SALINITY: the concentration of salts in dissolved water.

SCIENCE: a discipline aimed at asking questions and learning about the universe, with no practical applications necessarily expected. Such a discipline is called a basic science. Ecology is a basic science. There are also applied sciences, such as environmental science. Science and technology are interdependent.

TECHNOLOGY: tools or techniques, based on scientific knowledge, that enable people to accomplish something.

TECHNOSPHERE: all nonliving systems of Biosphere 2 that make it function, such as the underground part of Biosphere 2 where most life-support and recycling technologies are located.

American Association for the Advancement of Science. 1993. *Benchmarks for Scientific Literacy, Project 2061:* Oxford University Press.

American Forest Council. 1987. *Project Learning Tree.*

Arizona Department of Education. 1985. *Arizona Teachers Resource Guide for Environmental Education.*

Arizona Department of Education. 1990. *Arizona Comprehensive Health Essential Skills.*

Arizona Department of Education. 1990. *Arizona Dance Essential Skills.*

Arizona Department of Education. 1990. *Arizona Dramatic Arts Essential Skills.*

Arizona Department of Education. 1993. *The Arizona Environmental Education Framework.*

Arizona Department of Education. 1987. *Arizona Essential Skills for Mathematics.*

Arizona Department of Education. 1987. *Arizona Essential Skills for Music.*

Arizona Department of Education. 1989. *Arizona Literature Essential Skills.*

Arizona Department of Education. 1990. *Arizona Science Essential Skills.*

Arizona Department of Education. 1989. *Arizona Social Studies Essential Skills.*

Arizona Department of Education. 1988. *Arizona Visual Arts Essential Skills.*

Arizona Department of Education. 1989. *The Language Arts Essential Skills.*

Barrett, James M. and Peter Abramoff, A. Krishna Kumaran, and William F. Millington. 1985. *Biology.* Prentice-Hall.

Brooks, J.G. and Martin G. Brooks. 1993. *In Search of Understanding: The Case for Constructivist Classrooms.* Association for Supervision and Curriculum Development.

Brown, L.R., Editor. 1992. *State of the World.* W.W. Norton & Company.

Daniel, Joseph E. (Ed.). 1992. *1992 Earth Journal—Environmental Almanac and Resource Directory.* Buzzworm Books.

EarthWise Environmental Learning Series. 1992. *Earth's Oceans,* Vol. I, No. 3. WP Press.

EarthWise Environmental Learning Series. 1992. *Sunlight,* Vol. I, No. 2. WP Press.

EarthWise Environmental Learning Series. 1993. *Energy,* Vol. I, No. 4. WP Press.

Gardner, Howard. 1993. *Multiple Intelligences: The Theory in Practice*. Basic Books.

Gates, David M. 1985. *Energy and Ecology*. Sinauer Associates, Inc.

Gentry, Linnea. 1993. *Inside Biosphere 2: The Ocean and Its Reef*. The Biosphere Press.

Gentry, Linnea and Karen Liptak. 1991. *The Glass Ark: The Story of Biosphere 2*. Penguin Books.

Goodman, Jan H. 1992. *Group Solutions*. University of California.

Harmin, Merrill, Ph.D. 1994. *Inspiring Active Learning*: Association for Supervision and Curriculum Development.

Hawkes, Nigel and Nigel Henbest, Graham Jones, Robin Kerrod, Terry Kirby, John H. Stephens and Nigel West. 1990. *How in the World?*. The Reader's Digest Association, Inc.

Kaler, James B. 1992. *Stars*. Scientific American Library.

Lapedes, Daniel N. (Ed.). 1978. *McGraw-Hill Dictionary of Scientific Terms*. McGraw-Hill, Inc.

Lapo, Andrey. 1987. *Traces of Bygone Biospheres*. Synergetic Press.

Leakey, Richard and Roger Lewin. (1992). *Origins Reconsidered*. Anchor Books.

Mitchell, Mark. K. and William B. Stapp. 1994. *Field Manual for Water Quality Monitoring*. Thomson-Shore, Inc.

Moore, Michael. 1989. *Medicinal Plants of the Desert and Canyon West*. Museum of New Mexico Press.

Odum, Eugene P. 1989. *Ecology and Our Endangered Life-Support Systems*. Sinauer Assoc., Inc.

National Science Teachers Association. 1991. *Science Education for Middle Level Students*, An NSTA Position Statement. Science Scope.

National Science Teacher's Association. 1992. *Scope, Sequence and Coordination of Secondary School Science*, Volume II, Relevant Research. NSTA.

National Science Teacher's Association. 1993. *Scope, Sequence and Coordination of Secondary School Science*, Volume I, The Content Core. NSTA.

New York Academy of Sciences, The. 1993. (Chapters by H.I. Modell and R.G. Carroll). *Promoting Active Learning in the Life Sciences Classroom*. Annals of the New York Academy of Sciences.

Niehaus, Judy H. 1994. *Learning by Frameworking—Increasing Understanding by Showing Students What They Already Know*. Journal of College Science Teaching, Vol. XXIV, No. 2, November 1994.

Rossi, Robert J. 1994. *Schools and Students at Risk*. College Teachers Press, Teachers College, Columbia University.

Scientific American. 1993 (E.O. Wilson, M.L. Lowe Chapters). *Managing Planet Earth*. Scientific American.

Sieloff, Debra and Brad Joseph. 1993. *Occupational Medicine: State of the Art Reviews*. U.S. Department of Health & Human Services.

Sieloff, Debra A. 1995. *The Powersphere™ Experiment Book*. HSP.

Sieloff, Debra. 1993. *The Technology Awareness Program*. UAW-Ford National Education, Development & Training Center.

Smith, Robert Leo. 1992. *Elements of Ecology*. Harper-Collins.

Spoon, Don 1994. *The Biosphere* Magazine Vol. 1, No. 2.

Terborgh, J. 1992. *Diversity and the Tropical Rain Forest*. Scientific American.

Texas Education Agency. 1993. *Environmental Essential Elements Across the Curriculum*.

Time-Life Books II Series. 1988. *Stars*. Time-Life Books.

U.S. Environmental Protection Agency. 1992. *The Consumer's Handbook for Reducing Solid Waste*. EPA.

Vernadsky, Vladimir. 1986. *The Biosphere*. Synergetic Press.

Walker, Richard. 1991. *Environment on File*. Facts on File.

Wasik, John F. 1993. *The Green Supermarket Shopping Guide*. New Consumer Institute.

Western Regional Environmental Education Council. 1992. *Project WILD*.

Wilke, Richard J. 1993. *Environmental Education Teacher Resource Handbook*. Kraus International Publications.

World Resources Institute. 1994. *World Resources 1994-95: A Guide to the Global Environment*. World Resources Institute.

Most Biosphere Press books listed in this reference are available for purchase.
Call for information • TOLL FREE (800) 992-4603

From Biosphere 2 & HSP. . . .

If you enjoyed this program, try the Power Sphere™. It's an experiment station that permits young people to do hands on research to discover the power of plants, light, water, soil, air and how the earth works. The 64-page activity book, included in the kit, was developed at Biosphere 2 by D. Sieloff and G. Dundas. **It's available at Biosphere 2.**

BIOSPHERE 2

POSTER SET

BIOSPHERE 2

RAIN FOREST

SAVANNAH

DESERT

MARSH

OCEAN

INTENSIVE AGRICULTURAL BIOME

MICRO CITY